fahd Shah
Nasir Khan Muhammad

EXPLORING THE EFFECTIVENESS OF ASSESSMENT METHODS

fahd Shah
Nasir Khan Muhammad

EXPLORING THE EFFECTIVENESS OF ASSESSMENT METHODS

Noor Publishing

Imprint
Any brand names and product names mentioned in this book are subject to trademark, brand or patent protection and are trademarks or registered trademarks of their respective holders. The use of brand names, product names, common names, trade names, product descriptions etc. even without a particular marking in this work is in no way to be construed to mean that such names may be regarded as unrestricted in respect of trademark and brand protection legislation and could thus be used by anyone.

Cover image: www.ingimage.com

Publisher:
Noor Publishing
is a trademark of
Dodo Books Indian Ocean Ltd. and OmniScriptum S.R.L publishing group

120 High Road, East Finchley, London, N2 9ED, United Kingdom
Str. Armeneasca 28/1, office 1, Chisinau MD-2012, Republic of Moldova, Europe
Printed at: see last page
ISBN: 978-620-7-47901-6

EXPLORING THE EFFECTIVENESS OF ASSESSMENT METHODS AT PRIMARY LEVEL

By

Shah Fahd

Dr. Muhammad Nasir Khan

ABSTRACT

This study was designed to analyze the continuous classroom assessment at primary level in Pakistan. Findings of the study revealed that the students' achievement of single class teacher in the subject of English, General science, Urdu and mathematics were almost on average and rubric observation during continuous classroom assessment ranked single class teacher performance fair. Overall, subject teacher students' achievement in English, General science, Urdu and Mathematics was better as compared to single class teacher. In addition to this, rubric observation during continuous classroom assessment ranked as subject teacher performance was reported very good in the area of students' instruction, writing test items on the writing board, time management, class environment, use of instructional recourses and student record keeping during and after assessment. It was recommended that at primary level, there is need of subject wise teacher to teach students more effectively. It is also recommended that primary teachers should be familiar with the new curricular terms such as Student Learning Outcomes (SLOs) used in curriculum 2006 and they can be trained to develop and use the new assessment tools that is, rubric in the classroom.

Table of Contents

CHAPTER 1

INTRODUCTION

Every stat nation has some aims and objectives for the development of its citizens these aims and objective are mainly achieved through an effective education system but to know the extent of achievement of these objectives, a proper assessment system is also needed Teacher is the main responsible figure in the whole education system who can assess the achievement To equip science with methods and techniques of assessment this course on assessment in science education has designed.

Assessment feedback reflect the learning setting and should be used to adjust course content teaching techniques or learning strategies to improved student science learning moreover the assessment data should be used to craft appropriate teaching professional development experiences and identify student who need extra help and or learning goals and instructional setting.

The majority of teacher in Pakistan unable to find to final out the Reason of poor teaching and learning process. Education system in Pakistan following summative assessment system majority of its institution the exam is held once or awarded system The use of this assessment method teacher do not know how to improved student learning skill the assessment is an ongoing process in which teacher and student both need to know the success of learning process with explicit feedback during the instructor.

.

1.1.1 Effects of Classroom Assessment on Student Achievement

In educational research, often large positive effects of teachers' use of classroom assessment on student achievement have been reported (studies reviewed in Black (wiliam 1998, 2013) or more recently in (Briggs et al.2012, 2012). Notwithstanding the fact that scholars of these studies in most cases refer to classroom assessment or formative assessment when they discuss their research, the similarity of the operationalization they opted for is quite low; many different definitions and assessment methods have been used under the same umbrella term of classroom assessment (2014, 2014) .

What strings studies on classroom assessment together, however—in addition to the terminology used—is that most interventions are focused on enhancing teachers' subject knowledge and promoting the use of assessments, thus allowing teachers to subsequently provide formative feedback to students. Formative feedback means "information communicated to the learner that is intended to modify the learner's thinking or behavior for the purpose of improving learning" (shute, 2007,2007) This type of feedback has been found to be most effective for motivating students and improving their learning In addition to the fact that the research projects on the effects of classroom assessment and their interventions were small scale, their comparability has been criticized because of the different conceptualizations of what classroom assessment entails (e.g., Bennett (2011, 2011)Even though the specificities of studies that have shown the effect of classroom assessment are different, their results do point to the effectiveness of the use of classroom assessment for improving students' mathematics achievement.

On the basis of such empirical results, recently, in the USA, the National Council of Teachers of Mathematics (Bennett, 2013) strongly endorsed teachers using classroom assessment strategies in their daily instruction in mathematics education. The basic idea behind the effectiveness of teachers' use of classroom assessment is that it can lead to teachers gaining more relevant and useful information on their students' understandings and skills. This allows them to subsequently better adapt their teaching to their students' needs, which in turn is expected to lead to improved student achievement.

A recent study with 45 primary school teachers in Sweden (2017, 2017) confirmed this line of reasoning with a yearlong intensive professional development program on using formative assessment strategies, resulting in students of these teachers significantly outperforming students in the control group on a mathematics posttest.

1.1.2 Formative assessment

Definition and characteristics of formative assessment term formative assessment is not used consistently in the literature (Bennett 2011). This has resulted in a number of definitions of formative assessment. The way in which 154 (2014) 26:153–176 these definitions are understood, interpreted and manifest in practice often reveals misunderstanding of the principles that the original ideals sought to promote (Klenowski, 2009)2009). Particularly, some authors see all classroom assessment as formative and discuss summative assessments primarily in terms of external assessments.

Other authors agree all classroom assessment can be formative, but only if teachers and students use the information for formative purposes, while others recognize that some classroom assessment can serve summative purposes too. Moreover, some authors claim that formative assessment refers to an instrument (e.g., Pearson 2005), as in a diagnostic test or an item bank from which teachers might create those tests (Wiliam and Thompson 2008), whereas educators and researchers argue that formative assessment is not an instrument but a process. In this view, the process produces not so much a score, but a qualitative insight into student understanding (Shepard 2008).

Taken together as (Bannet, 2011) argues, formative assessment might be best conceived as neither a test nor a process, but some thoughtful integration of process and purposefully designed methodology. Another term used almost interchangeably with formative assessment is that of assessment for learning. Black et al. (2003) make a distinction between these two terms by arguing that assessment intended to promote learning only becomes formative when evidence is actually used to adapt teaching work to meet learning needs. In addition, another term that is often confused or used interchangeably with formative is that of diagnostic assessment.

An assessment could be considered as diagnostic when it provides information about what is going amiss and formative when it provides guidance about what action to take (thompson, 2008). It is also important to note that not all diagnostic assessments are instructionally actionable. Black (1998, p.26) offers a somewhat different view, stating that: ' diagnostic assessment is an expert and detailed enquiry into underlying difficulties, and can lead to a radical re-appraisal of a pupil's needs, whereas formative assessment is more superficial in assessing problems with particular classwork, and can lead to short-term and local Change in the learning work of a pupils.

1.1.3 Classroom based learning

Classroom based learning (CBL) is continuous monitoring of student behavior motivation attitude, learning style and teaching strategies during a class (CBL) is not only assessment of student and his achievement but also critically analyses teaching techniques and strategies if reaching. Assessment is also used in selection controlling or motivating student and to satisfy public expectation as to standards and accountability (Biggs2003p141)

Consequently, or summative depending on how the result are used. The formative assessment also help teachers are having judge and improved the skills of pupils it also proved information on the effectiveness of teaching which will help to determine an appropriate remedial action where Necessary and summative assessment takes a place at the end of course or program to determine the level of student achievement or how well a program has performed.

1.1.4 Formative and summative assessment

Formative assessment take place where teacher and student respond to students work judgment about what is good learning with feedback information about how the student present state of learning and how the student mane actual outcome relates to goal and standards desired outcome relates to goals and standards.(Dick, 2009.2006).

The idea that dialogue is fundamental to successful learning and teaching is well documented in the education literature and research have acknowledged that formative assessment can play a central role in shaping and improved the effectiveness of the teacher learning experience civic and (joues, 2008,2007)

Summative assessment the other hands creates tests academic report and qualification which are socially highly valued Biggs, (2003) summative assessment also designed to help make (final), judgment about a learners' achievement on a program and potential subsequence achievement and certify achievements.

Learner then any type of any assessment conducted outside the classroom. Absolumetal,2009 classroom assessment are particularly important to improved student learning especially where the comprise formative feedback and help student to understand their own learning strategies this means that in country with effective student assessment greater emphasis is placed on what happen in classroom and the role of the teacher Clarke (20/2).Critical component in determining student progress at the primary level the teacher also know by the help of assessment the class level him and Adams (2023

1.1.5 Definition and characteristics of formative assessment

The term formative assessment is not used consistently in the literature (Bennett 2011). This has resulted in a number of definitions of formative assessment. The way in which 154 Educe Asser Ace (2014) 26:153–176 these definitions are understood, interpreted and manifest in practice often reveals misunderstanding of the principles that the original ideals sought to promote (Klenowski, definition and characteristic of formative assessment , 2009). Particularly, some authors see all classroom assessment as formative and discuss summative assessments primarily in terms of external assessments.

Other authors agree all classroom assessment can be formative, but only if teachers and students use the information for formative purposes, while others recognize that some classroom assessment can serve summative purposes too. Moreover, some authors claim that formative assessment refers to an instrument (e.g., Pearson 2005), as in a diagnostic test or an item bank from which teachers might create those tests (Willams, 1998), whereas educators and researchers argue that formative assessment is not an instrument but a process (Pelham 2008).

In this view, the process produces not so much a score, but a qualitative insight into student understanding (Shepard 2008). Taken together, as Bonnet (2011) argues, formative assessment might be best conceived as neither a test nor a process, but some thoughtful integration of process and purposefully designed methodology.

Another term used almost interchangeably with formative assessment is that of assessment for learning. Black et al. (2003) make a distinction between these two terms by arguing that assessment intended to promote learning only becomes formative when evidence is actually used to adapt teaching work to meet learning needs. In addition, another term that is often confused or used interchangeably with formative is that of diagnostic assessment. An assessment could be considered as diagnostic when it provides information about what is going amiss and formative when it provides guidance about what action to take ((Thompson, 2008).

It is also important to note that not all diagnostic assessments are instructionally actionable. Black (1998, p.26) offers a somewhat different view, stating that: '… diagnostic assessment is an expert and detailed enquiry into underlying difficulties, and can lead to a radical re-appraisal of a pupil's needs, whereas formative assessment is more superficial in assessing problems with particular classwork, and can lead to short-term and local changes in the learning work of a pupil.

Such problems of definition are often further confounded by external policy changes (see for example, Pollard et al. 1994; Torrance and Pryor 2001).

Thus, it is important to distinguish formative assessment from other current interpretations of classroom assessment. Most authors agree that assessment can be considered formative only if it results in action by both the teachers and students to enhance learning (Black and Wiliam 2006). For the purposes of this study, we adopted the definition of formative assessment provided by the Assessment Reform Group in the UK (2002, pp.1–2) as "the process of seeking and interpreting evidence for use by learners and their teachers to decide where the learners are in their learning, where they need to go and how best to get there".

In order to make the differences clear, it is useful to summarize the basic characteristics of formative assessment. According to Black and William (2009), formative assessment can be conceptualized as consisting of five key strategies:

(1) clarifying and sharing learning intentions and criteria for success; (2) engineering effective classroom discussions and other learning tasks that elicit evidence of student understanding; (3) providing feedback that moves learners forward; (4) activating students as instructional resources for one another; and (5) activating students as the owners of their own learning. Additionally, other characteristics found in the literature refer to formative assessment as an ongoing multi-process, integrated in the teaching and learning, that is carried out on a daily basis through teacher-pupil interactions.

In this process, teachers modify their instruction and activities, according to the assessment information, in order to improve learning processes and student outcomes. As Black et al. (2003) argue, formative assessment applies not to the assessments themselves, but to the functions they serve in supporting students' learning and providing evidence that is used to adapt the teaching to meet learning needs.

Taking this functional view, successful implementation of formative assessment depends on the learning approach and teachers' knowledge, skills and strategies that they use to carry out complex pedagogical processes (Webb and Jones 2009). From this perspective, several studies demonstrated that, while formative assessment is desirable, it is not easy for teachers to achieve (e.g. Torrance and Pryor 2001; Marshall and Drummond 2006).

1.1.6 Problems in effective implementation

Although there is a growing literature reporting positive effects of formative Assessment upon teaching practice and students' outcomes, there is also a growing literature on the difficulties of introducing formative assessment in ordinary classroom settings. For example, Hall and Burke (2003) have found that although teachers perceived positively formative assessment and acknowledged its importance, they faced several difficulties in implementing effectively formative assessment practices in their classrooms.

Consistent with these findings, both the National Research Council (1996) and the National Council of Teachers of Mathematics (2000) in the USA have recommended that teachers develop and use formative assessment practices on a systematic basis. As The Office for Standards in Education in England (OFSTED) supports, "Although the quality of formative assessment has improved perceptibly, it continues to be a weakness in many schools" (1998, Section 5.6).

Black (1996) also argues that formative assessment is still undervalued and underdeveloped. He claims that in Britain and in the rest of the world teachers do not use effective assessment practices while teaching. There are several reasons why successful implementation of formative assessment is still problematic, as elaborated below.

As discussed in the previous section, the various definitions and the consequent conceptual understandings of the concept have created a confusion of what formative assessment really implies in terms of classroom practices (Klenowski, definition and characteristic of formative assessment , 2009)Most teachers are familiar with summative assessment, and only few implement, effectively, formative assessment in their classrooms (Willams, 1998)

Several studies (e.g. Morgan 1996; Peerce and Skinner; 1999; Shen 2002) have shown how the summative assessment requirements dominate the assessment practice of many teachers. Particularly, in the context of USA primary classrooms, it was found that teachers do not distinguish between formative and summative purposes (Bashar and Anderson 1994), and based on these findings, Shepard's (2000) calls for a transformation of classroom assessment practices, to support and enhance learning.

Moreover, effective implementation of formative assessment requires the development of new tools and changing classroom practices (Black and William 2003). Such changes may be related to practical issues such as an increase in record keeping required in some formative assessment practices (MacPhail and Halbert 2005; Brookhart 2010).

In addition, formative assessment is difficult to achieve because empirically derived models of learning are not generally available and the shift in 156 Educ Asse Eval Acc (2014) 26:153–176 teacher practice required is large and may also involve changing teacher beliefs and values related to effective teaching and learning (Webb and Jones 2009).

In addition, the increasing policy emphasis on measuring academic standards and the need for evidence-based policy development has created a pervasive emphasis on summative evaluation for high stakes purposes. Although summative assessment has been subject to severe challenge and its ability to improve the teaching and learning process has been questioned (Black and Wiliam 2009), educational accountability today issynonymous with student achievement outcome testing and the sanctions that accompanythe results (Darling-Hammond 2004).

National educational policies internationally have moved forward to create approved level assessments and targets for schools, and students to make adequate yearly progress. In turn, such kind of national policies have pressed individual schools to meet student achievement targets on summative large-scale evaluations (Militello et al. 2010).

1.1 Rationale of the Study

Teaching and learning are interrelated processes. Not only they depend on each other but have immense affected on each other. Similarly, assessment and instruction are also related components. The feedback gained through assessment plays vital role in the adoption, rejection and adaptation of certain teaching strategies and methodologies.

The result of assessment is not only grading of students' achievement but also help teacher to takes decisions for his teaching styles. Since last couple of decades, there have been revolutionary changes in the system of education. Besides focusing on the learning behaviors and attitudes of students, researchers are also emphasizing on the teachers' part within getting guidance and teaching process.

It is for that reason professional development related to teachers is considered as the crucial element for the education system. According to (pestieau, 1995) the instructor's growth as a professional teacher achieves with a result to gain the increased experiences as well as investigating either his or her teaching in as systematic way.

The teacher is regarded as thoughtful expert, who come in the occupation with one's basic familiarity to improve it with his experiences and new knowledge gained (lyte, 2011) This idea of improving skills and knowledge through experiences is only possible through classroom based assessment, where you can get students' responses on the spot and reflect on the teaching styles and strategies in perspectives of the students' performance. For that purpose, knowing how to examine and what to examine is most important factor.

Unfortunately, in Pakistan there is lack of such professional development centers and institutes for teachers in general and for assessment as specific (Villegas-Reimers, 2003.2003) shed light on different issues in the assessment system of Pakistan and concluded that assessment and examination system in Pakistan has more demerits than merits. Institutes like Agha Khan University, Society of Pakistani English Language Teachers and Higher Education Commission of Pakistan are taking efforts in this direction but they are not in access of all Pakistani teachers.

1.2 Statement of problem

The help of assessment method the also judge the learner abilities also use the different assessment tool use the test, quiz, interview, question and answer section, though which the teacher also judge the learner abilities.

Measurement the learner abilities and also use the different assessment method like the formative assessment which the teacher uses during the class to judge the learner abilities and thought and the use of summative assessment, the main focus of assessment the guide the teacher that how to use the assessment method. The assessment method main goals to measure the leaner capabilities and ideas about the subject like diagnostic assessment the teacher also use to judge the pervious knowledge.

1.3 Objective

To develop the learner abilities use the different assessment.

With the help of formative assessment achieve the learner aim and objectives.

To probe the different ways of using Tabs for the student assessment in the primary level.

To explore the benefits of using Tabs for the teachers in the primary level school context.

How do the Tabs use for the student's assessment in the primary level schooling context?

What are the benefits of using the Tabs for the teachers in primary level school context?

1.4 Research Question

To probe the different ways of using Tabs for the student assessment in the primary level.

To explore the benefits of using Tabs for the teachers in the primary level school context.

How do the Tabs use for the student's assessment in the primary level schooling context?

What are the benefits of using the Tabs for the teachers in primary level school context?

Which assessment mostly use in primary level classroom for the development of learner abilities and ideas?

How the classroom based assessment (CLB) can helpful for the development of learner abilities?

1.5 Significance of problem

The supplementary level of data would be providing the powerful forthcoming into the crash and significance of effectiveness of assessment through tabs at the primary level. Student's assessment is very vital to make the teaching-learning process more effective and efficient.

There are number of ways to assess students, one of way is the use of Tabs to assess the student's learning outcomes. In this connection, the statement of problem is designed to explore the "effectiveness of assessment through tabs at primary level" to attain desired outcomes and how do the teachers use Tabs for assessment of concerned students.

1.6 Delimitation of study

The delimitation of the study were to

Primary school level

Primary school student

Islamabad

CHAPTER 2

LITERATURE REVIEW

The debate of Classroom based assessment started with the publication of Black and, (Willams, 1998)phenomenal article on classroom formative assessment. The study of opened the new spheres in assessment strategies and fetched interest of academicians and researchers towards classroom-based assessment (CBA) and its potential for enhancing learning. In order to understand the phenomenon of Classroom based assessment, it is essential to understand the relationship between learning, teaching and assessment techniques used (perron, 2011).

It is through implementing various strategies of assessment that teachers collect information about the success or failure of their teaching styles, methods or decision making about the classroom instructions A (purpure, 2009) according to the information collected in assessment and observations determines the confirmation of comprehension and learning gaps in classroom; hence, teachers subsequently incorporate more intervening and improvised teaching strategies.

2.1 Teacher & Classroom Based Assessment

Although the research has acknowledged the importance of learner in assessment, (Andrade, 2010)it is nonetheless recognized that teachers still have an important part to play in the process (Purpura, 2009). Hence, the importance of teacher has gained increasing concerns towards using assessment for accountability purposes (Leung & William 2014; Malone, 2013) as well as the widespread introduction of policies to implement assessment-for-learning principles in curriculum and assessment (Fulcher, 2012,2014) These developments have focused attention on teachers' capacity to deliver assessment reforms, with teacher assessment literacy (TAL) identified as a critical factor in improving student learning (Hattie, 2012).

2.1.1. Role of CBA in Language Acquisition

The importance of Classroom based assessment has not only been acknowledged in learning and comprehension (cheng, 2005,2001) but has also been examined as main factor in to promote second language acquisition (Redickens, 2008)A lot of research has been conducted on the impact of CBA on EFL learners and second language acquisition (perron, Research artical , 2011) 2006, 2007, 2009; Re-Dickens, 2001, 2004, 2013). A detailed study of these researches will enable teachers to comprehend the relationship between CBA and language learning and acquisition.

Most state certification systems and ha lf of all teacher education programs have no assessment course requirements, nor they do have an explicit requirement that teachers have received training in assessment (wise, 1992,2000,1991). Soon after, Bloom (1968) and Bloom, and Hasting (1971) took up this idea, applying the concept to student assessment in their work on "mastery learning".

They initially proposed that instruction be broken down into successive phases and students be given a formative assessment at the end of each of these phases. Teachers would then use the assessment results to provide feedback to students on gaps between their performance and the "mastery" level, and to adjust their own teaching to better meet identified learning needs (Allal, 2005).

2.2 Classroom based assessment in Pakistan

(Warsi, 2004,2006), termed the assessment system in Pakistan as examination of rote memorization. According to them, the language assessment in Pakistan is not assessing or testing the concrete skills of students but it is the test of their cramming.
Whereas the objectives of the examination and the nature of assessment determines the approaches of teaching and learning (Rehmani, 2003). The primary objective of an assessment is towards facilitating processes of teaching and learning by gaining feedback from the results (Rehmani, 2003)argued in his study on public examination in Pakistan that assessment in Pakistan will play significant role if it is conducted for the improvement of education, teaching learning approaches and it is only possible with the blend o f summative and formative assessment.

Similarly, L.D Fink (2003) proposed a model of course designing emphasizing that assessment should be the main element of any course design and it is critical for students and teachers to know whether the goal is teaching is accomplished or not. Fink (2003) argued that assessment is not only the tool of "Audit-ive assessment" to assign only grades but should be "Educative assessment" to measure whether students got it and teacher realized his/her weakness and strength in teaching process.

English, being the official and foreign language in Pakistan has critical role in educational, professional and official system. Hence, learning of English has become vital part in society and named as social symbol by researchers (Rehmens , 2008'2011). So, the understanding and training of Classroom based assessment can be beneficial for both students and ESL teachers.

2.3 Types of assessment method

A comprehensive assessment process include three types of assessment they are Implemented at different points in a lesson pre assessment is used at the beginning of a lesson or unit to determine student needs and or baseline level knowledge.

Formative assessment preformed over the course of lesson to determine student progress so that teacher can adjust instruction and student can reflect on their learning summative assessment is conducted at the end of a lesson to evaluate student learning and to promote teacher reflection on the effectiveness of the curriculum and instruction.

Traditional assessment is a form of summative assessment usually involving multiple choice true-false, short answer or essay question non-traditional assessment use additional approaches such a portfolios ,performance –based evaluation time-series design assessments predict and-explain assignments and concept mapping these approaches provide more comprehensive measure of student cognitive abilities (wright, 2001) and are often more successful in measuring the student abilities integrate concepts and perform specific skills.

2.3.1. Peer assessment

The peer assessment where the teacher give the opportunity to learner collaborative with his friends and achieve the knowledge form one to the other and also improve peer learner also develop the abilities of pupils.

2.3.2. In-School/Classroom Assessments

The ESA indicates that classroom-level formative assessments of learning are practically non-existent or, at best, reduced to one six monthly and one annual examination testing memory only, not whether students are learning basic skills.

The ESA traces this to that forces teachers to teach to memory-based tests, lack of teacher understanding about assessments and how to use them, and the unrealistic course length which teachers are more concerned about completing than in learning.

2.3.3. O Large-Scale Assessments:

Established in (o large-scale assessment , 2016) as a statutory authority, thePakistan Assessments and Examination Commission (BAEC) is responsible for conductinglarge-scale sample-based diagnostic assessments and high-stakes summative examinationsat the end of primary (Grade 5) and middle (Grade 8) schools. However, currently BAEC only conducts examinations at Grade 8 level.

Moreover, there are concerns that these large-scale examinations at primary and middle levels may not be effective since they are focused less on learning and more on grading students for continuation to the next level of education. Since BAEC was only recently established it is in the processing of developing its capacities and has therefore not yet started any diagnostic assessments that could provide feedback into the teaching and learning process.

The BAEC also lacks institutional and human resource capacity to fulfil its mandate by developing and overseeing implementation of coherent and aligned assessment framework with relevant tools and capacity building of teachers and supervisors and ensuring that the classroom based formative assessments, school based summative assessments and large scale sample based diagnostic assessments are conducted according to a coherent learning design and provides relevant information at different levels for decision making.

The natural corollary to the above is that the education system lacks coherence and direction. It should be focusing on learning outcomes if it is to be effective – the only real 6 measure of a quality input is whether students learn what they are supposed to learn, i.e. the basic skills of reading, writing, comprehension, critical analysis and mathematics. This requires assessments and feedback of each input and process to know whether it contributes to these results.

The low participation rates in Pakistan are due to a number of factors. These include insufficient number and poor distribution of schools, local access-related challenges poor learning in classrooms which discourages enrolment and retention, and limited availability of post-primary opportunities. For girls, there is less school availability than for boys at every level.

Girls' schools comprise 27 per cent of total primary schools, 41 per cent of middle schools and 33 per cent of secondary schools. Transitioning to post-primary, and even persisting to the end of primary school, is less likely when no accessible middle schools are available.

In some areas, national schools are already full or overcrowded, and do not have the capacity to absorb refugee children. The lack of basic amenities and conducive classroom environments also contributes to high dropout rates, particularly for girls, children with disabilities and refugees. The ESA finds that 83 per cent of schools do not have drinking water. Primary schools constitute the largest share of such schools. The situation of sanitary facilities is also poor, with almost 71 per cent of schools lacking toilets.

In schools with large student populations, the functionality, maintenance and cleanliness of toilets is a major problem. These factors are already detrimental to student retention, and are likely to worsen considering the COVID-19 pandemic. Underlying all these sector issues are both institutional (including processes) and individual capacity weaknesses.

Assessment is a critical component in determining students' progress at the primary level. It is an essential tool that will produce a progress report and a recapitulation of the topics and knowledge given to the students. A class (al, 2002)teacher can know the level of understanding of the students eloquently through an assessment (adms H. a., 2013). Assessment phenomena aid in motivating students by assessing their grasp of the subject as well as their level of cognition. Adequate knowledge of assessment techniques benefits both students and teachers because the course of assessment reveals the teacher's strengths and weaknesses (adms, 2002).

The assessment method the also highlight three major objective of assessment there also come common effects which also define by (Stiggin, 2008)the also define the assessment method according to the three major assessment method education assessment for the learner use of different assessment method like the formative assessment method which the teacher also use the continuously monitor the success levels of the student based on the learner objectives.

(adms H. a., 2013) mention that "it is up to the teacher to create an active classroom environment that optimizes learning for students with quite different abilities and interest

The also more define it that the use of peer assessment we also developed the learner abilities and also improved the ideas and thought attitude behavior and thinking capabilities or also improved and develop new skills or talent in learner.

The classroom based assessment method start with the publication of the (william, 2019) also define the formative assessment method that use during class when the teacher teach learner the also use the formative assessment essential port of student knowledge develop and also make between teacher and student the co relationship. The formative assessment method is also a phenomenon that to develop the learner ideas and thought use of same assessment tools the assessment tool are use in different strategies to enhance the learner abilities and also bring the changes in learner abilities with help of assessment method.

The formative assessment also based on three main element through which the teacher also asses the learner ideas and motivate the pupils to learn. The formative assessment method also have big role to judge the learner abilities according to (perron, classroom basid assessment method, 2011)the also define the teaching learning strategies to bring the implement the learner ideas and make a collaboration with learner to promote the styles and collect the information about the learner success and failures of teaching techniques.

According to the (purpore, 2009 2007), the also define the assessment method to judge the learner abilities and also improved the skills and observe the learner that how the student have interest in class lecture and they are not shying in class or the focusing or not with the help of formative assessment method and the also find the gaps of learning that what are the gaps.

2.4 Teacher & Classroom Based Assessment

Although the research has acknowledged the importance of learner in assessment, (Andrade, 2010), it is nonetheless recognized that teachers still have an important role to develop the learner abilities the also a main part to play in the process (purpore, 2009). Hence, the importance of teacher has gained increasing concerns towards using assessment for accountability purposes and also bring the new techniques and improvements (malone, 2014.2013) as well as the widespread introduction of policies to implement assessment-for-learning principles in curriculum and assessment (Fulcher,2012;).

These developments have focused attention on teachers' capacity to deliver assessment reforms, with teacher assessment literacy (TAL) identified as a critical factor in improving student learning. (Hatti, 2013).

2.4.1 Classroom Based Assessment in Pakistan

(warsi, 2004)(kenan, 2006) , the assessment system in Pakistan there also use the assessment method like summative assessment method like as a examination of rote memorization. According to them, the language assessment inductive method in Pakistan is not assessing or testing the concrete skills of students but it is the test of their cramming. Whereas the objectives of the examination and the nature of assessment determines the approaches of teaching and learning process the teaching and learning process is two way process one is form the teacher to the learner and from the learner to the teacher (Rehmani, 2003).

The primary objective of an assessment is towards facilitating processes of teaching and learning by gaining feedback from the results (Rehmani, 2003) argued in his study on public examination in Pakistan that assessment in Pakistan will play significant role if it is conducted for the improvement of education, teaching learning approaches and it is only possible with the blend of summative and formative assessment. Similarly, L.D Fink (2003) proposed a model of course designing emphasis that assessment should be the main element of any course design and it is critical for students and teachers to know whether the goal is teaching is accomplished or not. Fink (2003) argued that assessment is not only the tool of "Additive -assessment" to assign only grades but should be "Educative assessment" to measure whether students got it and teacher realized his/her weakness and strength in teaching process.

2.4.2 Summative assessment

The summative assessment according to (Hashmi) takes place at the end of large chunk of learning with the results being primary for the teacher or school use Results may take time to be returned to the student, feedback to the student is usually, and the student usually has no opportunity to be reassessed. Thus summative assessment tends to have the least impact on improving an individual students understanding or performance student parent can use the result of summative assessment to see where the student's performance lies compared to identify strength and weaknesses of curriculum and instruction.

2.4.3 Continues vs terminal (or final) assessment

This is not so much a method as an indication of and how often assessment is made, continuous assessment was introduce party because of complains that it was unfair and unnecessary stressful to learner to know that they were being examined on only a single occasion or over a short period of time where luck with the question played a particularly significant part in their chances of success.

2.4.4 Coursework vs Examination

Although continuous assessment is more likely to be of coursework. It could incorporate the result of tests and even examination grades tend to enjoy greater respectability in the eye of the public then coursework grades

2.4.5 Process vs product assessment

Teacher are most accustomed to the assessment of products, most frequently those by children using pencil or pen on paper or their equivalent. This kind of outcome is of great important such as essay, technical drawings and so on. in those subjects, where product are not the goal, assessment tends to be avoided such as contemporary religious education where ability to discuss and to appreciate the points of view of others is encouraged. Process and product are intimately related. There would be no product without processes. Assessment of product is easy than assessment of process.

1. Rating scale

2. Observation /interaction schedules

3. Anecdotal records

4. Simulation method

2.4.6 Rating scale

A rating scale is a tool used for assessing the performance of tasks, skill level procedures, processes, end products, such as reports, drawings, and computer programs and behaviors and attitudes. Rating scale indicate the degree of accomplishment rather the just presence or absence of the trial assessed. To compose a rating scale in one column performance statements are given in other columns the scale is give indicating the range or level of achievement. In order to rate student's performance the procedure and processes are observed and the item on the list are checked.

2.4.7 Interaction schedule

What goes on in a classroom, how do students interact with each other and with teacher what has long been the focus of classroom studies. Classroom interaction studies are focused on the practices, processes and conditions to understand their relationship with learning and student achievement. The major goals of interaction studies are it.
The develop an observation schedule categories of student and teacher behavior (verbal and non-verbal) are identify keeping in view the purpose of the study and the teaching learning situation .

2.5 Assessment: what it entails

The word 'assessment' take its root for the Latin word 'assidere', meaning "to sit beside another." As the meaning of the word denotes, in education, teachers stand beside the students to understand the extent to which the students have achieved their learning goals.

Assessment is an important part of every learning process. It is a method used by the educators to understand the performance of the learners and it is of various forms. According to (Crick, 2002) assessment is a word used to describe any action by which indication of learning is gathered in a planned and an organized manner for the purpose of making judgment about learning. Meanwhile (Masters, 2014) believe that the ultimate purpose of educational assessment is to find and understand the position of learners with regard to their learning at the point of assessment.

For years summative form of assessment was mainly used in schools to understand the students learning. However, educators and policy makers realized that summative assessment alone is not sufficient to understand the progress of the students and inform the learning. This idea is also supported by stating the summative assessment is suitable when the assessment purpose is to summaries the learning for grading, certification or record of progress, but formative assessments are most appropriate when the assessment aim to facilitate for making decisions about the improvement of learning and making judgments regarding the next step in learning therefore, formative assessment is important for the development of the educational process.

According to (OEDC, 2008) formative assessment consists of frequent assessments of students which are interactive and which evidence the progress of students' learning that helps to understand learning needs of the students to bring adjustments to teaching process. Thus, it has to be an integral part of the teaching and learning process. Moreover, (Cambridge Assessment.

Also believes that, for the students' learning to be improved through meaningful feedback assessment for learning must be integrated into the teaching and learning process as it the tool that creates the opportunity to provide feedback for the students' on going learning. In addition to this, Cambridge Assessment International Education (2017) further encourages to apply the practices of assessment for learning as it strengthen the significance of the feedback process which confirm that the students' earning is maximized.

(Morover , 2012), argues that any classroom that focus on students, assessment and the instruction must go together hand in hand. (Regier, 2012) further believes that a range of different assessment strategies have to be applied by the teacher to explore the eagerness of the students to learn a certain unit of study and plan the instruction to accommodate the needs of the students. For this process it continue, ongoing assessment of the students is vital.

Therefore assessment for learning is essential approach to be applied through various forms and methods to enhance the students learning and to inform the teaching process for the purpose of making judgments, along with adjustments to the teaching process.

2.5.1 Definition of formative assessment

(Hargreves, 2005), the teacher and the learner. In her study, she posits that assessment for learning AFL involves thinking outside of traditional assessment practices and moving beyond the limitations of standardized testing. The author argues that AFL involves using assessment as a tool for learning, rather than simply measuring student performance, and that it can be used to enhance student motivation, engagement, and achievement.

Hargreaves discusses the importance of involving students in the assessment process and helping them to understand the criteria for success in their learning. He also emphasizes the need to provide timely and specific feedback that helps students to self-assess and set goals for improvement. The study highlights the importance of using a variety of assessment methods to gather evidence of student learning and the importance of aligning assessment practices with instructional goals.

Overall (Stiggins, 2005) defines formative assessment as a deliberate process in which teachers use assessment-generated evidence of students' progress to modify their ongoing instructional practices, or students use it to adjust their current learning strategies.

He argues that formative assessment can lead to success in standards-based schools, as it guides instruction and improves student achievement.

(Stiggins, 2005), asserts that assessment for learning AFL should focus on the needs of the learner, provide ongoing feedback to help students set goals for improvement, align with instructional goals, and incorporate multiple sources of evidence to gather information about student learning. This study emphasizes the importance of using AFL to guide instruction and promote student achievement, especially in standards-based schools.

2.5.2 Benefits of Formative Assessment

As any type of assessment, the formative assessment is characterized by some benefits that have been identified by various researchers. One of the main benefits of formative assessment is that it can help to improve student learning outcomes. Studies have shown that when teachers use formative assessment, students are more likely to achieve higher grades and improve their overall understanding of a topic (Black & wiliam , 1998)Another benefit of formative assessment is that it can help teachers to identify and address student misconceptions in real-time.

By using a variety of assessment methods, teachers can gain insights into what students know and understand, and use that information to guide their instruction and clarify misunderstandings (Clarke, 2005).

Hyland and (Hyland, 2006)tackled the concept of feedback in second language (L2) writing and provided a comprehensive discussion of the different types of feedback and its role in language learning. They argued that feedback in L2 writing should be seen as a dynamic and interactive process, rather than a one-way transmission of information from the teacher to the student. The authors also emphasized the importance of considering the context and culture in which the writing is produced, as well as the individual needs and preferences of the learners.

Overall, the study highlights the importance of effective feedback in promoting L2 writing development and suggests that formative assessment can be a valuable tool in achieving this goal. In this regard, (less, 2008) discussed the perspectives, practices, and problems of L2 writing teachers regarding error feedback. The study examined thepractices of error feedback and its challenges in two English as a second language (ESL) writing classes in the United States. The author aimed to provide insight into the factors that influence ESL writing teachers' feedback practices, including their beliefs, pedagogical goals, and contextual factors.

Study revealed that teachers' feedback practices were shaped by a range of factors, such as the type of writing task, the proficiency level of the students, and the teachers' beliefs about the effectiveness of feedback. The findings suggest that L2 writing teachers need to be more reflective about their feedback practices and consider their students' individual needs and learning styles when providing feedback.

Besides, another interesting study related to the role of formative assessment in L2 writing was done by (Shute, 2008). His study aimed at providing a comprehensive review of formative feedback in educational contexts. The author defines formative feedback as information communicated to the learner that is intended to modify learning and improve performance. The study explores the different types of formative feedback and their effectiveness in enhancing learning outcomes.

Shute discusses the importance of timely feedback, the role of self-assessment and peer assessment, and the importance of aligning feedback with learning goals. The study also provides recommendations for designing and implementing effective formative feedback in different educational contexts. Overall, the study highlights the importance of formative feedback in promoting learning and improving educational outcomes.

2.5.3 Primary teaching classroom assessment

In education, assessment plays a crucial role that helps teachers with reflective instruction while also measuring students' competence and learning in terms of their scores and grades. Within an official learner-centric education system, students are more affected by evaluation than they are by the instructor or the organization. The results of assessments may be impacted by a number of things. According to the learners, they could include psychological variables, memory, interest, and unique learning methods.

From an institutional perspective, variables may comprise the following: subject, kind of assessment, classroom setting, teaching style, instructors' assessment literacy, and assessment instruments (Deluca, 2019). However, it is undeniable that one important component in influencing the validity of assessment is teachers' assessment knowledge. The study used an experimental approach to find out the effect of professional development training in the assessment skills of teachers on their performance in assessment related tests.

Professional development Training and Assessment skills of Teachers
There are various issues involved in the failure of primary schools such as less qualified teachers, poor content knowledge, use of poor teaching methods and assessment techniques, and lack of professional development training (al K. e., 2011)

In another study, (Memon, 2007) criticized the low teaching quality and poor use of student assessment techniques as two wide-ranging problems of declining student performance. Ministry of Education (2009) endorsed that the modern assessment techniques have not ever been used to measure the students' achievement. The previous literature further also tells that the teachers generally use outdated teaching methods, the assessment takes place is sporadic and subjective, policy implementation is not successful and it provides little feedback to children for improvement (iqbal, (2009),(2015))

In Pakistan, (Butt, 2021) found that the various of reasons of failure for primary education system include memory-based assessment rather than testing analytical ability, endemic administrative issues in the conduct of examinations, and low teacher quality. Another study found that lack of financial resources, insufficient teaching staff and ineffective use of assessment techniques are the important indicators of low-quality teaching in Pakistan at primary level (al A. e., 2013).

Was concluded that, in overall, there were three wide-ranging problems poor student performance that needed to be resolved immediately such as poor subject matter knowledge of teachers, poor use of student assessment techniques, and poor use of the teaching strategies.

In certain situation, when the primary schools were failing and the Punjab government was paying billions of rupees to the caretakers of these failing schools, it was high time to provide trainings where possible, and suggest remedial actions so that the system could work effectively.

This research was initiated to address these challenges properly and find out the proper solutions to effective assessment skills and educational improvement of schools. There are various studies which confirmed the importance of professional development training to enhance the assessment skills of teachers and overall instructional process in education system.

(Christoforidou , 2021), conducted the study on developing teacher assessment skills through their professional development training which revealed that these types of trainings had great impact on both teachers' assessment skills and student learning. Similarly, Sato et al. (2008) examined the effect of professional development on the enhancement of assessment skills of teachers through using longitudinal approach. The study revealed that teachers were proficient in using different assessment techniques gradually through arranging the training on different occasions. In another study.

Assessing the Effectiveness of Differentiated Instruction Strategies in Diverse Classrooms. (Smale-Jacobse, 2019), state that in recent years, the need for differentiated instruction has grown more apparent due to the increased cultural and linguistic diversity, as well as the variety of learning styles and needs, in today's classrooms. Oftentimes, today's students come from a variety of cultural and linguistic backgrounds and may have varying learning styles, interests, and demands (Okaz, 2015).

Teachers must employ methods that account for individual variances if they are to successfully satisfy the needs of all students. Educators can select from a variety of methods that have proven effective in differentiating lessons for their students. Flexible grouping is one such method, in which students are placed in groups according to their individual needs and talents rather than their chronological age or grade level (al s.-H. e., 2016)

A teacher might pair up students who are having trouble with the same idea with those who already have a solid grasp of it in order to give each student individualized attention and help. The use of tiered assignments is another method that has proven successful in inclusive classrooms. This means offering a range of assignment difficulties so that each student can select one that is just right for them. Students who are having trouble grasping a certain idea might benefit greatly from this approach since they are given the freedom to work at their own pace while still receiving the necessary guidance.

Differentiating instruction in inclusive classrooms can also be accomplished through the use of multiple pedagogical approaches. According to (Syofyan, 2018), visual, aural, and hands-on approaches can all be effective, although some children may learn more effectively through one of these ways than another. When educators employ a wide range of strategies, they increase the likelihood that every student will be able to grasp the material presented.

To address the requirements of a wide range of students, differentiated education has been proved to be useful in the classroom. Teachers should regularly evaluate the success of their differentiated education methods and adapt them as necessary. As part of this process, you can ask for and use student and teacher feedback, as well as compile data on student progress to guide your teaching. All students, regardless of their cultural or language backgrounds, learning styles, or requirements, can benefit from a classroom in which teachers use a variety of varied instruction tactics and routinely review their efficacy.

CHAPTER 3

METHODOLOGY

Met by phenomenon being investigated. The basic assumptions guiding interpretative paradigm are that knowledge is socially constructed by the people active in the research process and the researchers should attempt to understand the complex world of lived experience from the point of view of those who live it.

3.1 Quantitative research

Many kind of essay question (those asking for things like the teacher opinion on a controversial issues, an analysis of a situation, or a free response interpretation of example of quantitative assessment.

3.2 Research design

This study is quantitative in nature. Method that was used to understand effectiveness of assessment through tabs at primary level is one-to-one given the closed ended question. In this connection, one of the advantages of qualitative methods in the form of closed ended question is that it become a vibrant conversation that can take different directions.

3.3 Random sampling

This research have used the random sampling and collected the information for selected samples. Following the process, 25 Islamabad based primary schools teachers, employing the random sampling, a sample method in probability sampling. For the data, the researcher applied the questioner method, close ended questions, and interviews, collated the appropriate data for the study.

3.4 Population & sample

Population in the research market comprises all the members of a defined group that you generalize to find the results of your study. This means the exact population will always depend on the scope of your respected study. Population in research is not limited to assessing humans; it can be any data parameter, including events, objects, histories, and more possessing a common trait. The measurable quality of the population is called a parameter. (Nicolas, 2021)

This research consisting the 44 primary school teachers (Mathematics, Urdu and Islamic studies) based in Islamabad as its overall population. These teacher were questioned about the effectiveness of different assessment method in primary school classroom in Islamabad, to know their general perspective.

3.5 Instrument & Data collection

Open-ended questionnaire was developed to explore the "effectiveness of Assessment through tabs at primary level". "The use of Questionnaire process of data collection in which the researcher gives the closed ended questions and records responses of a single participant in the study at the same time. The individual to meet and given them the closed ended questionnaire methods were adequate for this study because the study investigates the effectiveness of different assessment through tabs at the primary level. In this study, open-ended questionnaire was used that allow the participants to be flexible..

The tracking probes were also used, they help to obtain more in-depth information. Same described the probes as "secondary questions under each question the researcher asks for more information or to expand or clarify information". Closed ended questionnaire also given to the all teachers of primary school and collect data.

CHAPTER NO 4

DATA ANALYSIS

The data analysis looked for specific recurring themes and common responses. The transcribed interviews of each personal interview were listened to, reviewed and analyzed to become familiar with the data. The following ideas, words or common statements were highlighted.

Creswell (2008), emphasized the need for a "preliminary exploratory analysis" which consists of obtaining a general sense of the data, making annotations and deciding if there is enough data (Creswell, 2008; Yin; 2012 &). In this connection, transcripts from individual interviews provided the raw data for the analysis. The transcripts of the interview were carefully reviewed once again to develop theme.

Table 4.1

Your age

	Frequency	Percent	Valid Percent	Cumulative Percent
18 – 25	14	56.0	56.0	56.0
26 – 35	7	28.0	28.0	84.0
46 or onward	4	16.0	16.0	100.0
Total	25	100.0	100.0	

Table 4.1 describe that (56%) had totally age is above then 18 or that teacher of different sector school participation in investigation the effectiveness of different assessment In

primary school classroom. While (28%) had totally age of (16%) the table value of mean score is (28.0) is greater and favoure the statement. Whereas, the cumulative percent (100.0).

Table 4.2

Your gender

	Frequency	Percent	Valid Percent	Cumulative Percent
Male	21	84.0	84.0	84.0
Female	4	16.0	16.0	100.0
Total	25	100.0	100.0	

Table 4.2 describe that (84%) had totally M is above the 18 or that teacher of different sector school participation Gender. While (16%) had totally age of (84%) the table value of mean score is (16.0 is greater and favoure the statement. Whereas, the cumulative percent (100.0) at Significance level. Hence it was founded that the statement is accepted.

Table 4.3

Your resignation

	Frequency	Percent	Valid Percent	Cumulative Percent
Teacher	19	76.0	76.0	76.0
Student	6	24.0	24	100.0
Total	25	100.0	1 00.0	

Table 4.3 describe that (76. %) had totally that teacher of different sector school participation your resignation. While (24%) had totally student (76%) the table value of mean score is 76.0 is greater and favoure the statement. Whereas, the cumulative percent (100.0) at Significance level. Hence it was founded that the statement is accepted.

Table 4.4

Marital status

	Frequency	Percent	Valid Percent	Cumulative Percent
Married	15	60.0	60.0	60.0
Unmarried	10	40.0	40.0	100.0
Total	25	100.0	100.0	

Table 4.4 describe that the teacher (60%) are married the totally the teacher the (40%) percent are unmarried or the totally the all participation marital status. Valid percent (60%) and while the table value 100.0.

Table 4.5

Your city

	Frequency	Percent	Valid Percent	Cumulative Percent
Islamabad	17	68.0	68.0	68.0
Lahore	3	12.0	12.0	80.0
Karachi	2	8.0	8.0	88.0
Quetta	3	12.0	12.0	100.0
Total	25	100.0	100.0	

Table 4.5 describe that the teacher (68%) are located in Islamabad and the (12%) are located in Lahore and the (8%0 are located in Karachi or (12%) located in Quetta the Participation Your city. The totally the 100.0. or the value of table is 68.0.

Table 4.6

In your opinion, the assessment is most effective for identifying student strength and weaknesses

	Frequency	Percent	Valid Percent	Cumulative Percent
Never	2	8.0	8.0	8.0
Rarely	3	12.0	12.0	20.0
Sometime	4	16.0	16.0	36.0
Frequently	5	20.0	20.0	56.0
Always	11	44.0	44.0	100.0
Total	25	100.0	100.0	

Table 4.6 describe that the (8%) teacher are never use the assessment or (12%) teacher rarely use assessment and the totally the all teacher are (25%) and the In your opinion, the assessment is most effective for identifying student strength and weaknesses the (16%) teacher use it sometime or the (20%) frequently use it or the (44%) teacher always use the assessment method in classroom or the totally all 100.0 or the valid percent. 44 or the cumulative percent is 100.0.

Table 4.7

How often do you use peer assessment that student evaluate in your classroom to each other.

	Frequency	Percent	Valid Percent	Cumulative Percent
Rarely	1	4.0	4.0	4.0
Sometime	6	24.0	24.0	28.0
Frequently	6	24.0	24.0	52.0
Always	12	48.0	48.0	100.0
Total	25	100.0	100.0	

Table 4.7 describe that the teacher (4%) Rarely use the assessment method or the (24%) sometime and the (24%) frequently use (48%) always use the How often do you use peer

assessment that student evaluate in your classroom to each other. The valid percent 100.0 the totally in cumulative percent 100.0.

Table 4.8

How Self, Assessment method develop collaboration between the student evaluate, each other.

	Frequency	Percent	Valid Percent	Cumulative Percent
Rarely	2	8.0	8.0	8.0
Sometime	8	32.0	32.0	40.0
Frequently	7	28.0	28.0	68.0
Always	8	32.0	32.0	100.0
Total	25	100.0	100.0	

Table 4.8 describe the (8%) had rarely (32%) had sometime (28%) has frequently (32%) had always use How Self, Assessment method develop collaboration between the student evaluate, each other. The totally the cumulative percent 100.0

Table 4.9

How often do you use diagnostic assessment during class to observe your student previous knowledge?

	Frequency	Percent	Valid Percent	Cumulative Percent
Never	2	8.0	8.0	8.0
Rarely	3	12.0	12.0	20.0
Sometime	6	24.0	24.0	44.0
Frequently	8	32.0	32.0	76.0
Always	6	24.0	24.0	100.0
Total	25	100.0	100.0	

Table 4.9 describe that the (8%) had never (12%) had rarely (24%) had sometime (32%) had frequently (24%) had always. How often do you use diagnostic assessment during class to observe your student previous knowledge? Cumulative percent is 100.0. The gather the value of table and hence accepted that the statement is accepted

Table 4.10

How often do you use summative assessment at the end of subject or topic (e.g. Quizzes, project). In your classroom.

	Frequency	Percent	Valid Percent	Cumulative Percent
Never	1	4.0	4.0	4.0
Rarely	3	12.0	12.0	16.0
Sometime	3	12.0	12.0	28.0
Frequently	8	32.0	32.0	60.0
Always	10	40.0	40.0	100.0
Total	25	100.0	100.0	

Table 4.10 describe that (4%) had never (12%) had Rarely (12%) had sometime (32%) had frequently (40%) had always. How often do you use summative assessment at the end of subject or topic (e.g. Quizzes, project). In your classroom. The table cumulative percent 100.0.

Table 4.11
Do you use, combination of assessment method at a same time or you get well, rounded picture of student learning

	Frequency	Percent	Valid Percent	Cumulative Percent
Never	2	8.0	8.0	8.0
Rarely	1	4.0	4.0	12.0
Sometime	8	32.0	32.0	44.0
Frequently	4	16.0	16.0	60.0
Always	10	40.0	40.0	100.0
Total	25	100.0	100.0	

Table 4.11 describe that (8%) had never (4%) had rarely (32%) had sometime (16%) had frequently (40%) had always. Do you use, combination of assessment method at a same time or you get well, rounded picture of student learning. The cumulative percent 100.0.

Table 4.12

DO you find assessment method more effective for certain subject

	Frequency	Percent	Valid Percent	Cumulative Percent
Never	2	8.0	8.0	8.0
Rarely	3	12.0	12.0	20.0
Sometime	5	20.0	20.0	40.0
Frequently	5	20.0	20.0	60.0
Always	10	40.0	40.0	100.0
Total	25	100.0	100.0	

Table 4.12 describe that (8%) had never (12%) had rarely (20%) had sometime (20%) had frequently (40%) had always. DO you find assessment method more effective for certain subjects. The table values 0f cumulative percent 100.0.

Table 4.13

How the assessment method used and motivate student and promote a growth of leaners

	Frequency	Percent	Valid Percent	Cumulative Percent
Never	1	4.0	4.0	4.0
Rarely	4	16.0	16.0	20.0
Sometime	4	16.0	16.0	36.0
Frequently	5	20.0	20.0	56.0
Always	11	44.0	44.0	100.0
Total	25	100.0	100.0	

Table 4.13 describe that (4%) had never (16%) had rarely (16%) had sometime (20%) had frequently (44%) had always. How the assessment method used and motivate student and promote a growth of leaners. The value of table to cumulative percent 100.0

Table 4.14

Through the use of assessment method do you take engage the student in class work.

	Frequency	Percent	Valid Percent	Cumulative Percent
Never	2	8.0	8.0	8.0
Rarely	3	12.0	12.0	20.0
Sometime	8	32.0	32.0	52.0
Frequently	4	16.0	16.0	68.0
Always	8	32.0	32.0	100.0
Total	25	100.0	100.0	

Table 4.15 describe that (8%) had never (12%) had Rarely (32%) had sometime (16%) had frequently (32%) had always. Through the use of assessment method do you take engage the student in classroom work? The Table value is cumulative percent 100.0.

Table 4.15

When implementing different assessment method how do you consider drives method drivers learning style and abilities in your classroom.

	Frequency	Percent	Valid Percent	Cumulative Percent
Never	1	4.0	4.0	4.0
Sometime	6	24.0	24.0	28.0
Frequently	7	28.0	28.0	56.0
Always	11	44.0	44.0	100.0
Total	25	100.0	100.0	

Table 4.15 describe that (4%) had never (24%) had sometime (28%) had frequently (44%) had always. When implementing different assessment method how do you consider drives

method drivers learning style and abilities in your classroom. the table of values also put cumulative percent 100.0.

Table 4.16

Assessment method can effect on primary level school student?

	Frequency	Percent	Valid Percent	Cumulative Percent
Never	3	12.0	12.0	12.0
Rarely	4	16.0	16.0	28.0
Sometime	2	8.0	8.0	36.0
Frequently	9	36.0	36.0	72.0
Always	7	28.0	28.0	100.0
Total	25	100.0	100.0	

Table 4.16 describe that (12%) had never (16%) had rarely (8%) had sometime (36%) had frequently (28%) had always the Assessment method can effect on primary level school student. The table values is cumulative percent 100.0.

Table 4.17

How often do you communicate assessment result with parents or group works?

	Frequency	Percent	Valid Percent	Cumulative Percent
Never	1	4.0	4.0	4.0
Rarely	5	20.0	20.0	24.0
Sometime	6	24.0	24.0	48.0
Frequently	10	40.0	40.0	88.0
Always	3	12.0	12.0	100.0
Total	25	100.0	100.0	

Table 4.17 describe that (4%) had never (20%) had rarely (24%) had sometime (40%) had frequently (12%) had always. How often do you communicate assessment result with parents or group works? Table value is cumulative percent 88.0.

Table 4.18

In your opinion, how effective are performance-based assessments in measuring student understanding.

	Frequency	Percent	Valid Percent	Cumulative Percent
Never	2	8.0	8.0	8.0
Rarely	2	8.0	8.0	16.0
Sometime	3	12.0	12.0	28.0
Frequently	7	28.0	28.0	56.0
Always	11	44.0	44.0	100.0
Total	25	100.0	100.0	

Table 4.18 describe that (8%) had never (8%) had rarely (12%) had sometime (28%) had frequently (44%) had always totally 25. In your opinion, how effective are performance-based assessments in measuring student understanding. Table value cumulative percent 100.0.

Table 4.19

Do performance based assessment encourage deeper learning and critical thinking skills?

	Frequency	Percent	Valid Percent	Cumulative Percent
Yes	11	44.0	44.0	44.0
No	2	8.0	8.0	52.0
To same	4	16.0	16.0	68.0

	Frequency	Percent	Valid Percent	Cumulative Percent
No idea	3	12.0	12.0	80.0
Total respondent	5	20.0	20.0	100.0
Total	25	100.0	100.0	

Table 4.19 describe that (44%) had yes (8%) had No (16%) had to same (12%) had No idea the totally respondent 25 or the Do performance based assessment encourage deeper learning and critical thinking skills? The value of Table cumulative percent 100.0.

Table 4.20

How often do you involve students in self-assessment activities?

	Frequency	Percent	Valid Percent	Cumulative Percent
Yes	10	40.0	40.0	40.0
No	2	8.0	8.0	48.0
To same	6	24.0	24.0	72.0
No idea	2	8.0	8.0	80.0
Total respondent	5	20.0	20.0	100.0
Total	25	100.0	100.0	

Table 4.20 describe that (40%) had yes (8%) had No (24%) had to same (8%) had No idea the totally respondent 25 and How often do you involve students in self-assessment activities? Table values is cumulative percent 100.0.

Table 4.21

Do you believe self-assessment helps students become weaknesses?

	Frequency	Percent	Valid Percent	Cumulative Percent
Yes	12	48.0	48.0	48.0
No	3	12.0	12.0	60.0
To same	2	8.0	8.0	68.0
No idea	4	16.0	16.0	84.0
Total respondent	4	16.0	16.0	100.0
Total	25	100.0	100.0	

Table 4.21 describe that (48%) had yes (12%) had No (8%) to same (16%) had totally respondent and the total 25 and Do you believe self-assessment helps students become weaknesses? Table values is cumulative percent 100.0.

Table 4.22

Are there any challenges you face when implementing different assessment method?

	Frequency	Percent	Valid Percent	Cumulative Percent
Yes	10	40.0	40.0	40.0
No	2	8.0	8.0	48.0
To same	7	28.0	28.0	76.0
No idea	1	4.0	4.0	80.0
Total respondent	5	20.0	20.0	100.0
Total	25	100.0	100.0	

Table 4.22 describe that (40%) had yes (40%) had No (28%) had to some (4%) had no idea (20%) had total respondent. The total 25 and Are there any challenges you face when implementing different assessment method? Table values cumulative 100.0.

Table 4.23

Do you differentiate your assessment based on student learning style?

	Frequency	Percent	Valid Percent	Cumulative Percent
Yes	11	44.0	44.0	44.0
No	4	16.0	16.0	60.0
To same	3	12.0	12.0	72.0
No idea	5	20.0	20.0	92.0
Total respondent	2	8.0	8.0	100.0
Total	25	100.0	100.0	

Table 4.23 describe that (44%) had yes (16%) had No (12%) had to same (20%) had no idea (8%) had total respondent. The total 25. Do you differentiate your assessment based on student learning style? The table values cumulative percent 92.0.

Table 4.24

Do formative assessment provide immediate feedback to students?

	Frequency	Percent	Valid Percent	Cumulative Percent
Yes	8	32.0	32.0	32.0
No	3	12.0	12.0	44.0
To same	6	24.0	24.0	68.0
No idea	5	20.0	20.0	88.0
Total respondent	3	12.0	12.0	100.0
Total	25	100.0	100.0	

Table 4.24 describe that (32%) had yes (12%) had No (24%) to same (20%) had No idea (12%) had total respondent. The total 25 and Do formative assessment provide immediate feedback to students? The table values cumulative percent 88.0.

Table 4.25

The use of assessment method can develop the learning environment?

	Frequency	Percent	Valid Percent	Cumulative Percent
Yes	9	36.0	36.0	36.0
No	3	12.0	12.0	48.0
To same	5	20.0	20.0	68.0
No idea	4	16.0	16.0	84.0
Total respondent	4	16.0	16.0	100.0
Total	25	100.0	100.0	

Table 4.25 describe that (36%) had yes (12%) had No (20%) had to same (16%) had No idea (16%) total respondent and the total 25 participation The use of assessment method can develop the learning environment? Table values is 84.0.

Table 4.26

How the assessment method gives learner opportunity the learner?

	Frequency	Percent	Valid Percent	Cumulative Percent
Yes	10	40.0	40.0	40.0
No	2	8.0	8.0	48.0
To same	7	28.0	28.0	76.0
No idea	4	16.0	16.0	92.0
Total respondent	2	8.0	8.0	100.0
Total	25	100.0	100.0	

Table 4.26 describe that (40%) had yes (8%) had No (28%) had to same (16%) had No idea (8%) had total respondent the Total all 25 participation How the assessment method gives learner opportunity the learner? Table values 92%.

Table 4.27

Do the assessment help the teacher to measure the pupil abilities?

	Frequency	Percent	Valid Percent	Cumulative Percent
Yes	11	44.0	44.0	44.0
No	1	4.0	4.0	48.0
To same	5	20.0	20.0	68.0
No idea	6	24.0	24.0	92.0

Total respondent	2	8.0	8.0	100.0
Total	25	100.0	100.0	

Table 4.27 describe that (44%) had yes (4%) had No (20%) t0 same (24%) had No idea (8%) had total respondent the total participation 25 and Do the assessment help the teacher to measure the pupil abilities? The values of table is cumulative percent 100.0.

Table 4.28

The use of summative assessment teacher can achieve the learner result?

	Frequency	Percent	Valid Percent	Cumulative Percent
Yes	11	44.0	44.0	44.0
No	2	8.0	8.0	52.0
To same	4	16.0	16.0	68.0
No idea	7	28.0	28.0	96.0
Total respondent	1	4.0	4.0	100.0
Total	25	100.0	100.0	

Table 4.28 describe that (44%) has yes (8%) had No (16%) had To same (28%) had No idea (4%) had Total respondent Total participation 25 and The use of summative assessment teacher can achieve the learner result? The Table values is 96.0.

Table 4.29

Which assessment is best suited to gauge student progress over time?

	Frequency	Percent	Valid Percent	Cumulative Percent
Teacher - made quizzes	9	36.0	36.0	36.0
Exit tickets	4	16.0	16.0	52.0
Student self-reflection journals	4	16.0	16.0	68.0
Final exam	8	32.0	32.0	100.0
Total	25	100.0	100.0	

Table.29 describe that (36%) had teacher made quizzes (16%) Exit tickets (16%) had student self-assessment (32%) had Final exam the total all 25 participation in Which assessment is best suited to gauge student progress over time, the Table values is cumulative percent 68.0.

Table 4.30

For fostering student ownership of learning which assessment method is most valuable

	Frequency	Percent	Valid Percent	Cumulative Percent
Traditional grading system	5	20.0	20.0	20.0
Self-assessment with clear learning goals	13	52.0	52.0	72.0
Peer, grading without guidance	5	20.0	20.0	92.0
High-stakes standardized	2	8.0	8.0	100.0
Total	25	100.0	100.0	

Table 4.30 describe that (20%) had traditional grading system (52%) had self- assessment system (20%) had self- assessment with clear goals (20%) had peer grading without guidance (8%) had high-stakes standardized. Total participation 25 and For fostering student ownership of learning which assessment method is most valuable? Table result come in cumulative percent 100.0.

Table 4.31

When assessing student collaboration skills, which method is most appropriate?

	Frequency	Percent	Valid Percent	Cumulative Percent
Individual written assignment	5	20.0	20.0	20.0
Group project presentation with rubric	10	40.0	40.0	60.0
Teacher observation of individual participation	6	24.0	24.0	84.0
Interview base test to give the learner	4	16.0	16.0	100.0
Total	25	100.0	100.0	

Table 4.31 describe that (20%) had individual writing assignments (40%) had group project presentation with rubric (24%) had teaching observation participation (16%) had interview best test the total 25 participation and When assessing student collaboration skills, which method is most appropriate? The table values 84.0.

Table 4.32

How does the frequency and type of assessment influence student motivate and engagement in learning activities?

	Frequency	Percent	Valid Percent	Cumulative Percent
Formative assessment	5	20.0	20.0	20.0
Summative assessment	9	36.0	36.0	56.0

	Frequency	Percent	Valid Percent	Cumulative Percent
Diagnostic assessment	7	28.0	28.0	84.0
Self-Assessment	4	16.0	16.0	100.0
Total	25	100.0	100.0	

Table 4.32 describe that (20%) had formative assessment (36%) had summative assessment (28%) had diagnostic assessment (28%) had self-assessment. The total 25 participation How does the frequency and type of assessment influence student motivate and engagement in learning activities and the table values 100.0.

Table 4.33

How does the frequency peer assessment help for the development of learner abilities through the use of which idea of work Assessment?

	Frequency	Percent	Valid Percent	Cumulative Percent
Collaboration works	8	32.0	32.0	32.0
Individual works	7	28.0	28.0	60.0
By discussion	6	24.0	24.0	84.0
Group works	4	16.0	16.0	100.0
Total	25	100.0	100.0	

Bar Chart

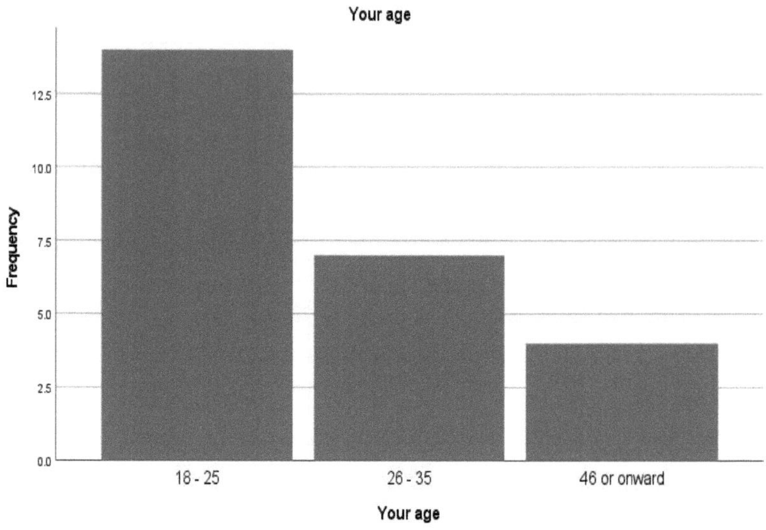

Your age
Frequency
12.5
10.0
7.5
5.0
2.5
0.0
18 - 25
26 - 35
46 or onward
Your age

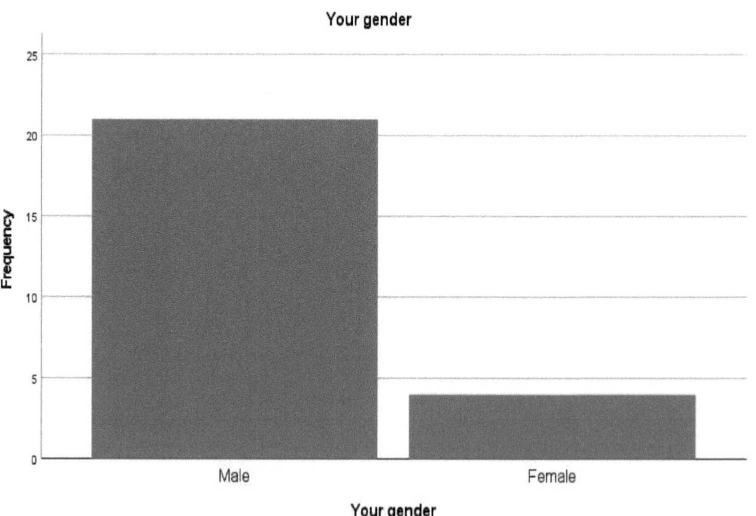

Your gender
Frequency
25
20
15
10
5
0
Male
Female
Your gender

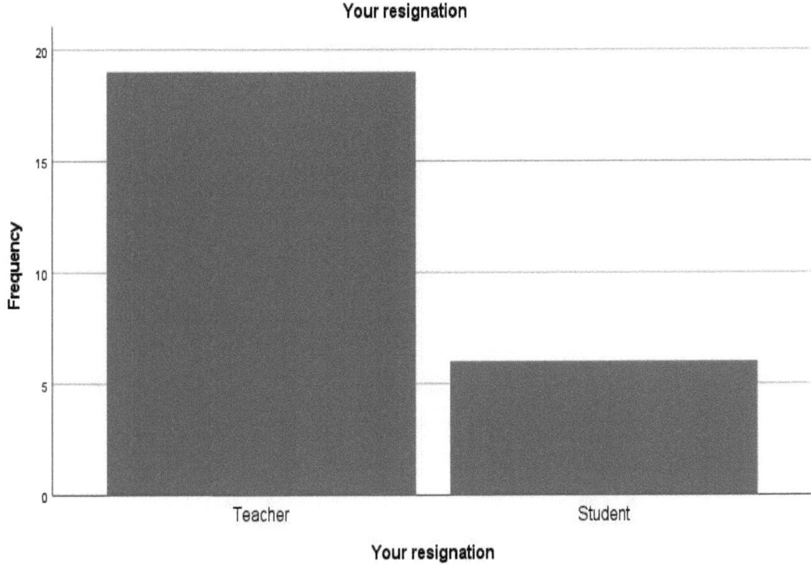

Your resignation
Frequency
20
15
10
5
0
Teacher
Student
Your resignation

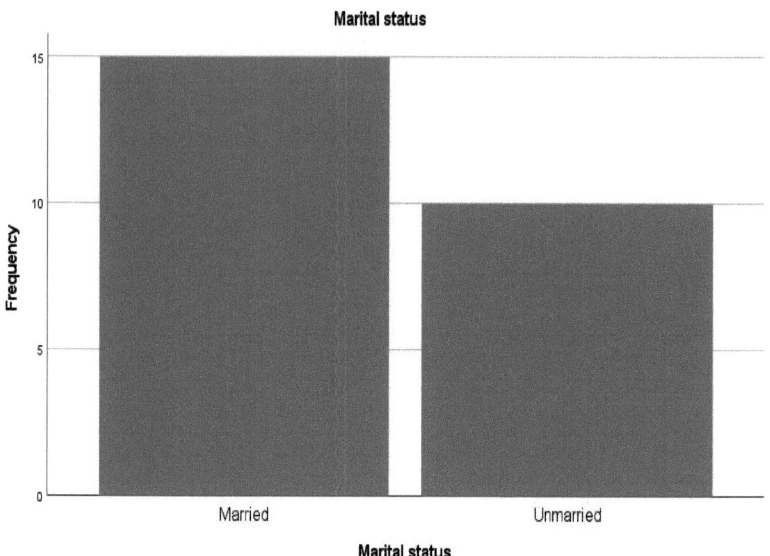
Marital status
Frequency
15
10
5
0
Married
Unmarried
Marital status

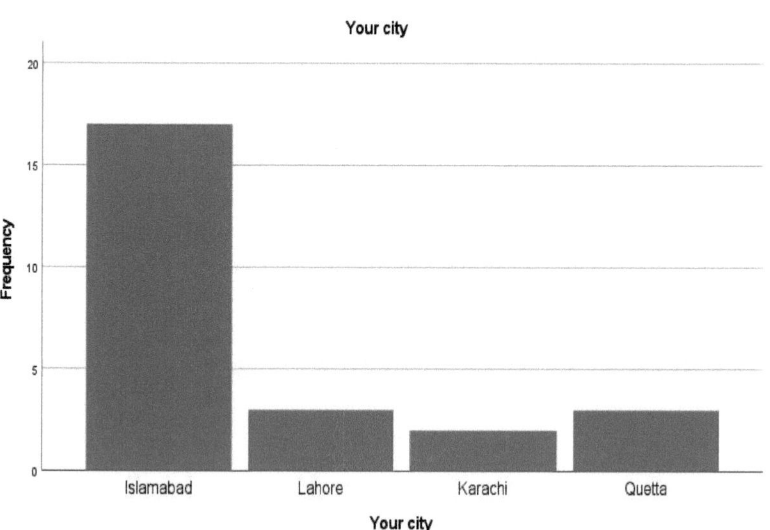
Your city
Frequency
20
15
10
5
0
Islamabad
Lahore
Karachi
Quetta
Your city

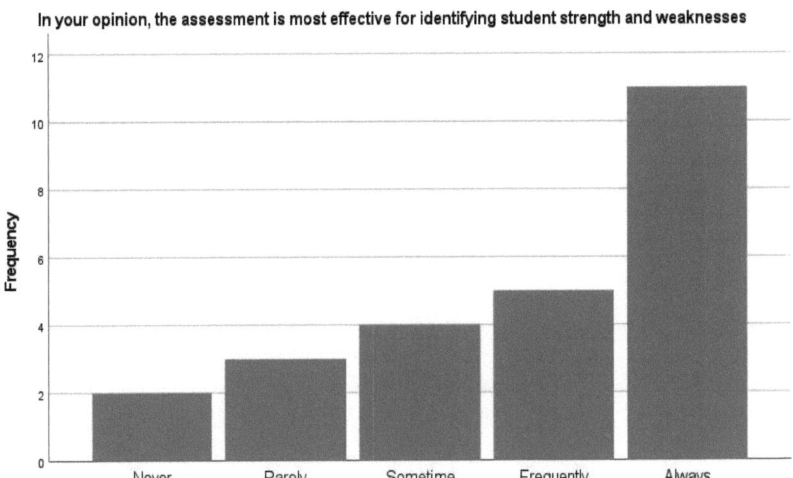

In your opinion, the assessment is most effective for identifying student strength and weaknesses

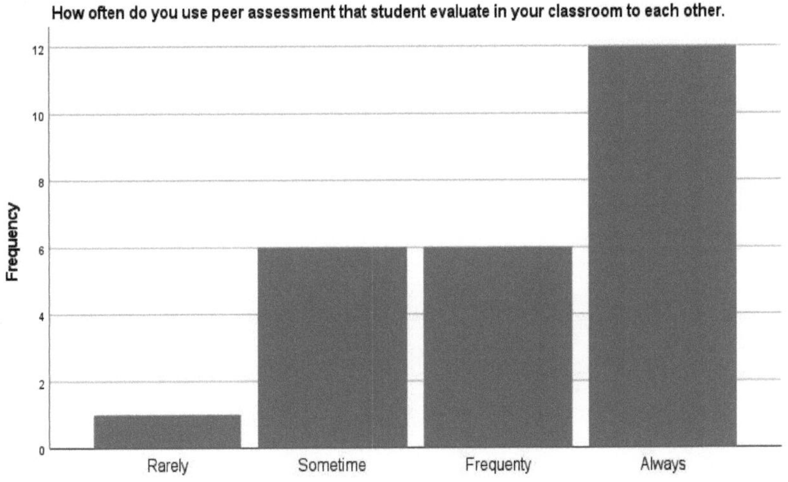

How often do you use peer assessment that student evaluate in your classroom to each other.

How Self, Assessment method develop collaboration between the student evaluate, each other.

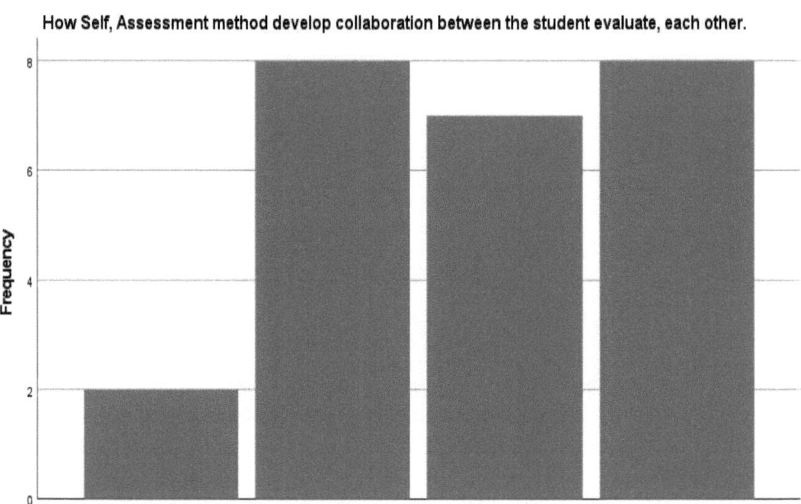

How Self, Assessment method develop collaboration between the student evaluate, each other.

How often do you use diagnostic assessment during class to observe your student previous knowledge

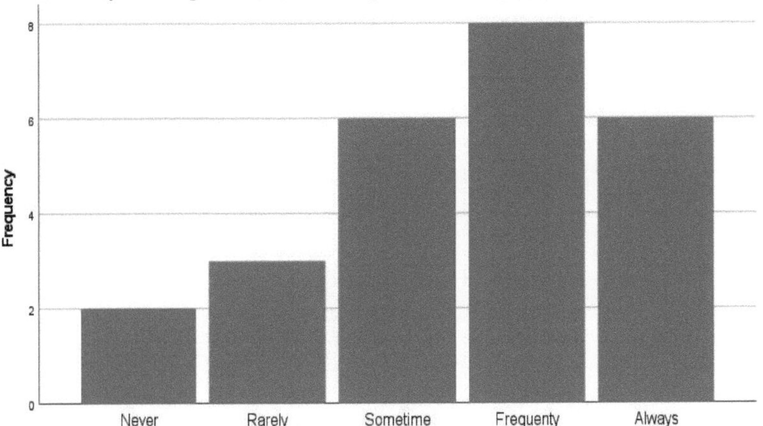

How often do you use diagnostic assessment during class to observe your student previous knowledge

How often do you use summative assessment at the end of subject or topic (e.g. Quizzes, project). In your classroom.

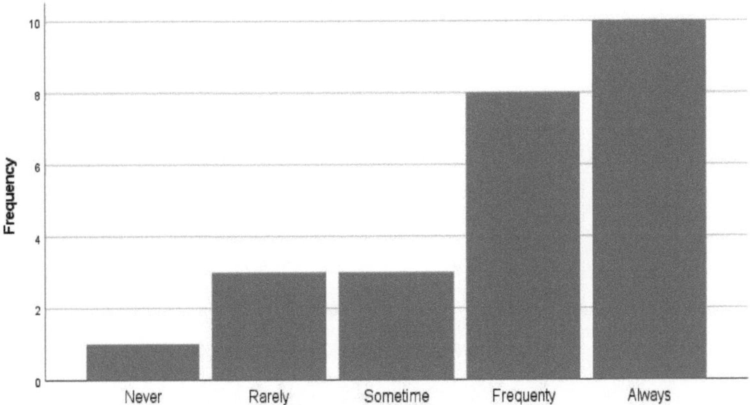

How often do you use summative assessment at the end of subject or topic (e.g. Quizzes, project). In your classroom.

Do you use, combination of assessment method at a same time or you get well, rounded picture of student learning

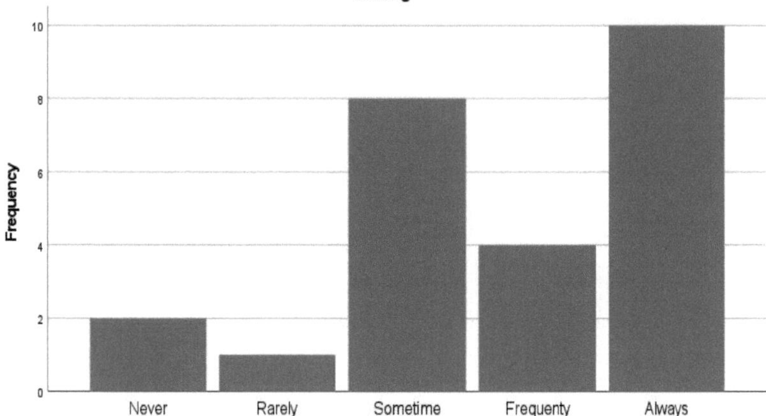

Do you use, combination of assessment method at a same time or you get well, rounded picture of student learning

DO you find assessment method more effective for certain subject

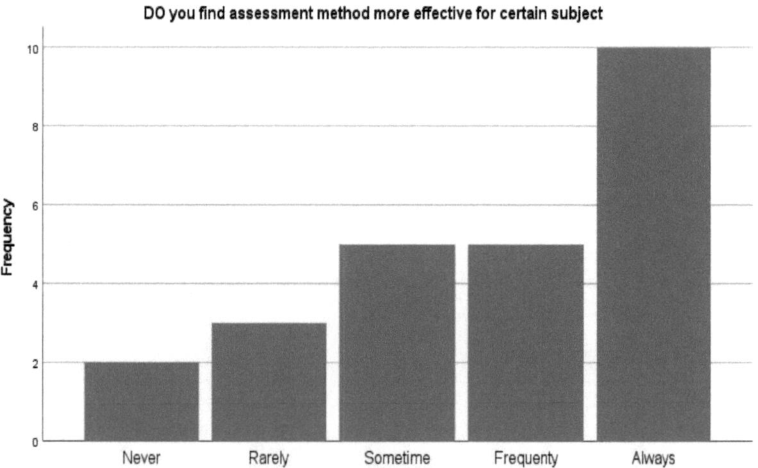

DO you find assessment method more effective for certain subject

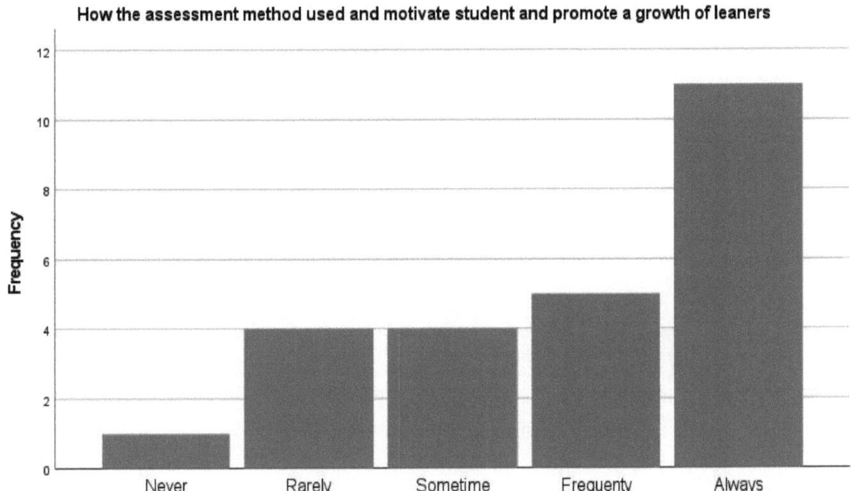

How the assessment method used and motivate student and promote a growth of leaners

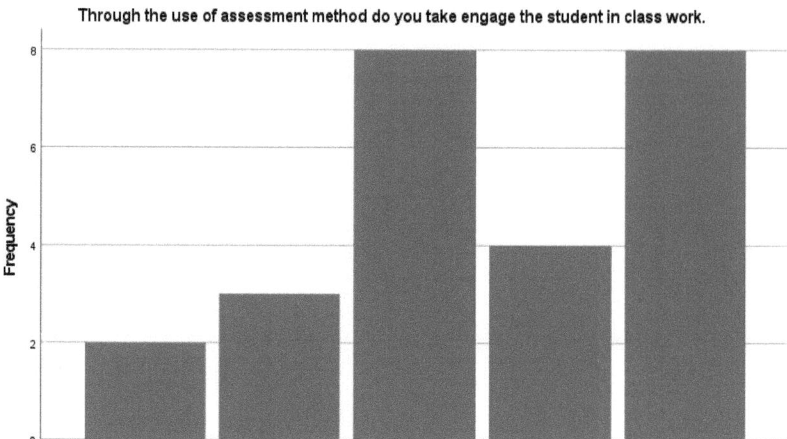

Through the use of assessment method do you take engage the student in class work.

When implementing different assessment method how do you consider drives method drivers learning style and abilities in your classroom.

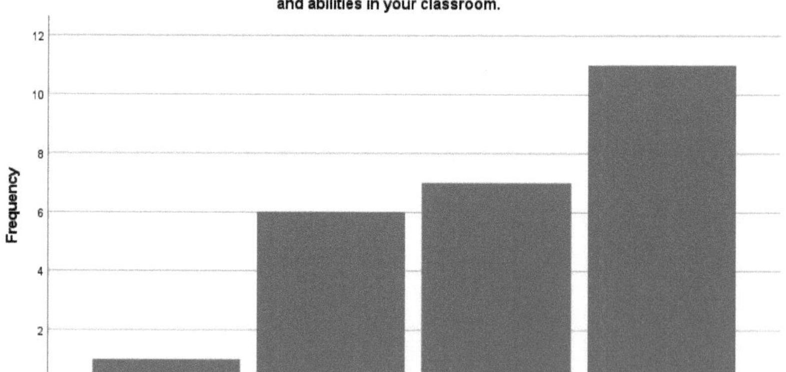

When implementing different assessment method how do you consider drives method drivers learning style and abilities in your classroom.

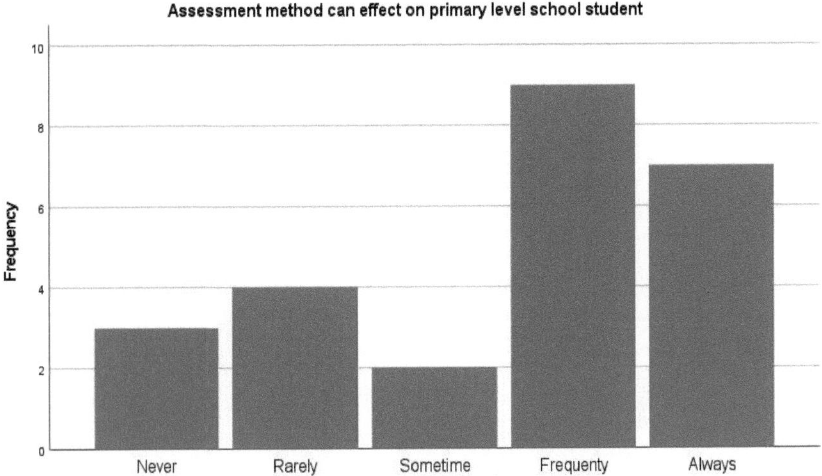

Assessment method can effect on primary level school student

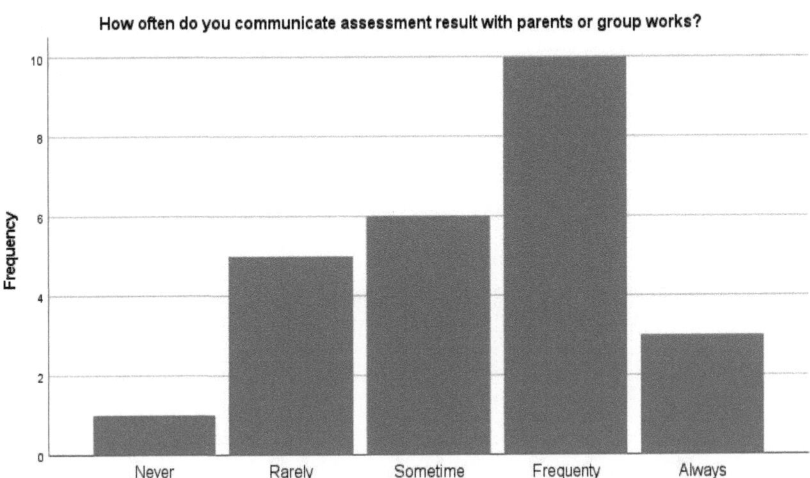

How often do you communicate assessment result with parents or group works?

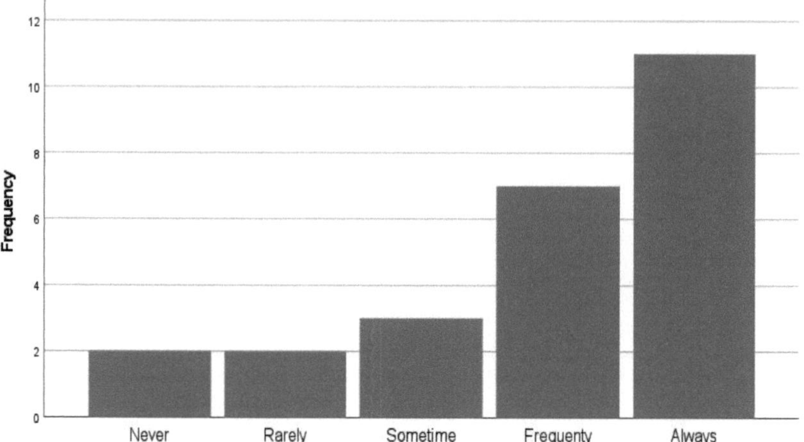

In your opinion, how effective are performance-based assessments in measuring student understanding.

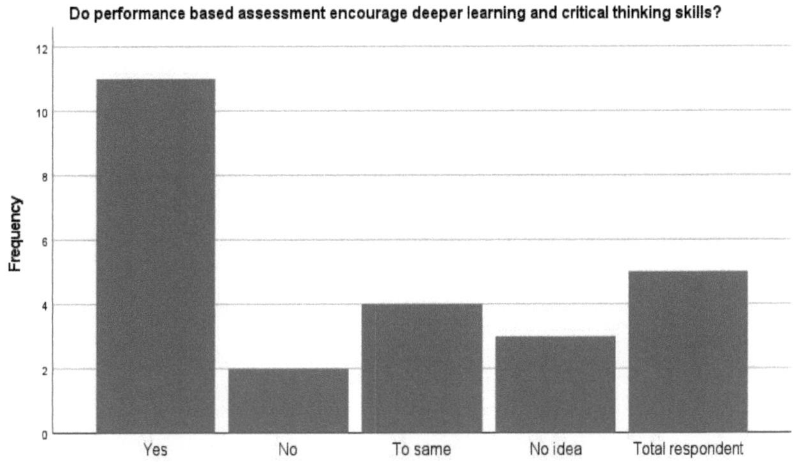

Do performance based assessment encourage deeper learning and critical thinking skills?

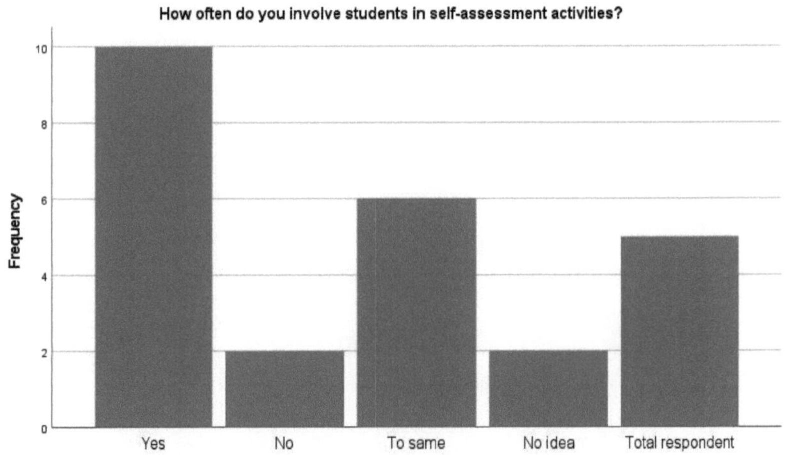

How often do you involve students in self-assessment activities?

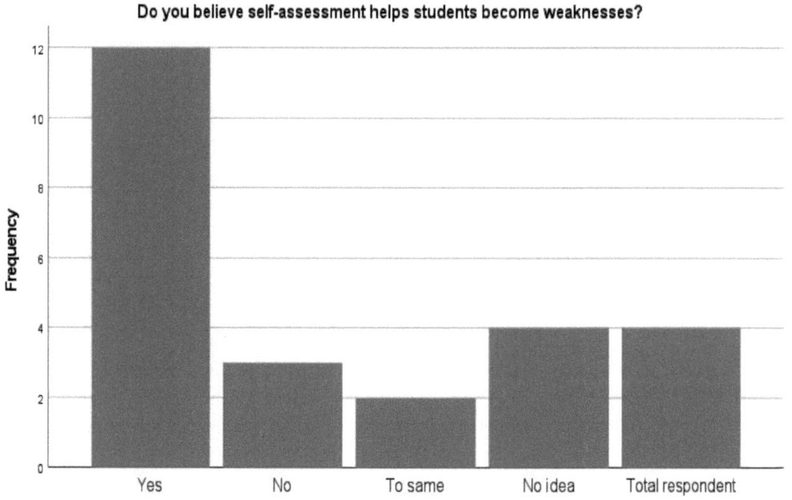

Do you believe self-assessment helps students become weaknesses?

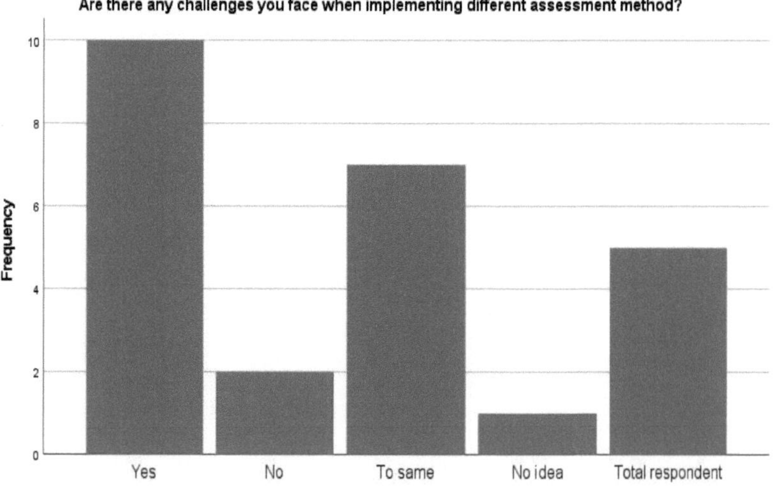

Are there any challenges you face when implementing different assessment method?

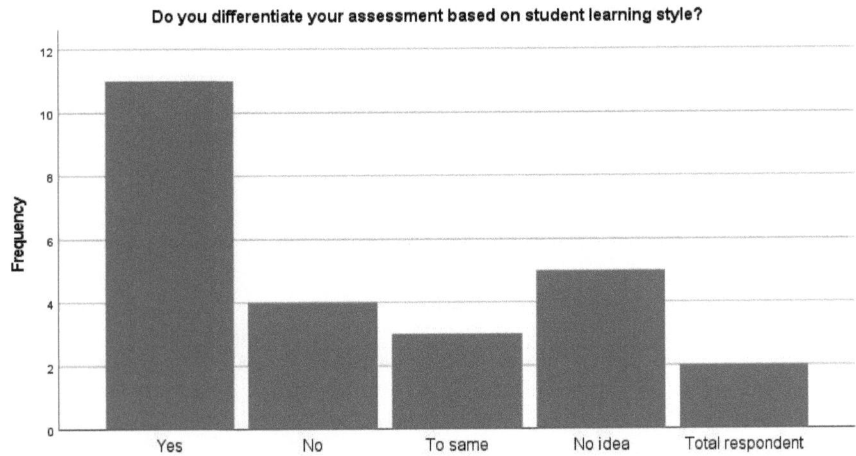

Do you differentiate your assessment based on student learning style?

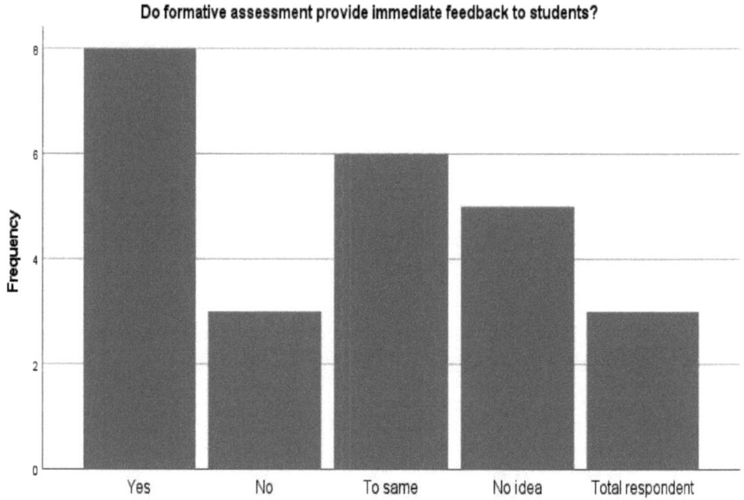

Do formative assessment provide immediate feedback to students?

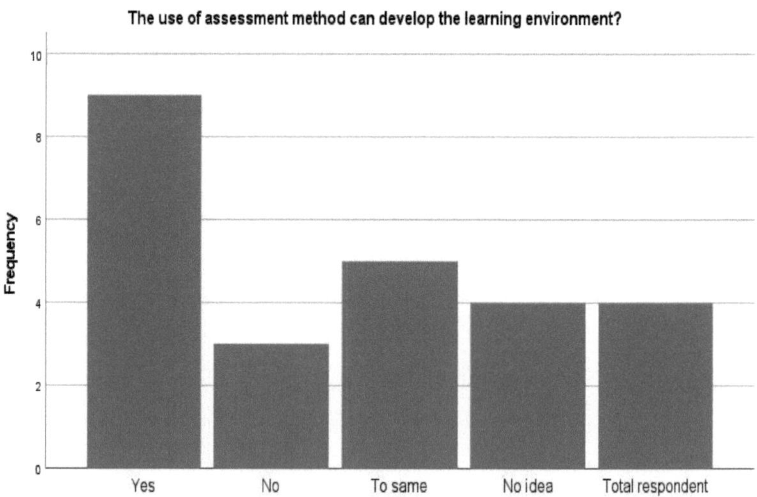

The use of assessment method can develop the learning environment?

How the assessment method gives learner opportunity the learner?

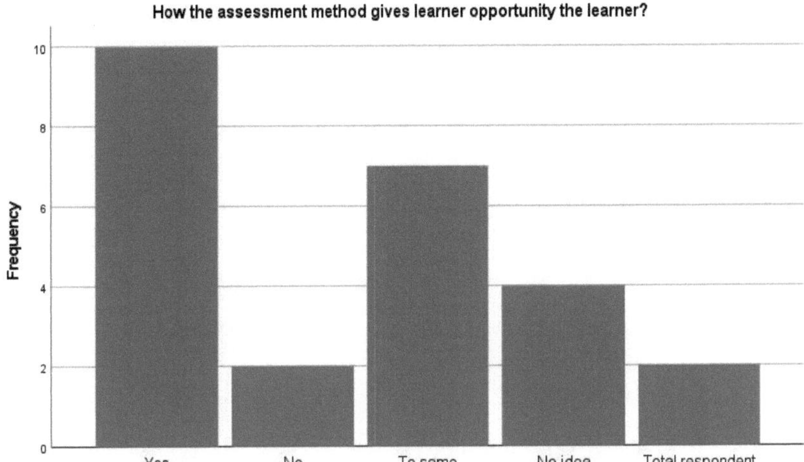

How the assessment method gives learner opportunity the learner?

Do the assessment help the teacher to measure the pupil abilities?

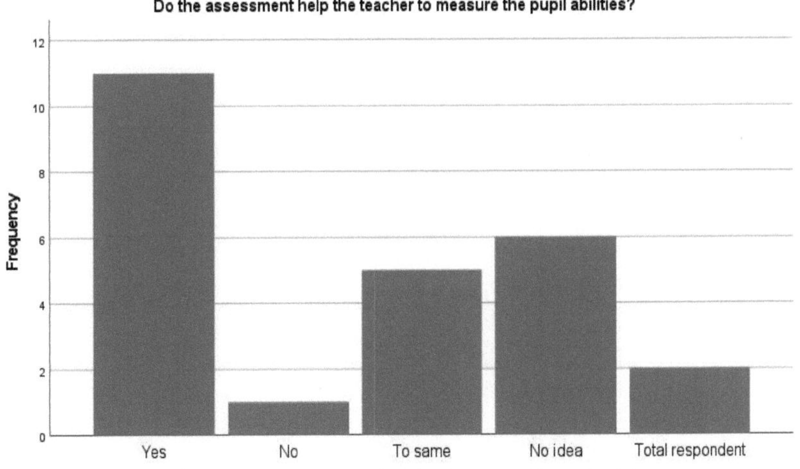

Do the assessment help the teacher to measure the pupil abilities?

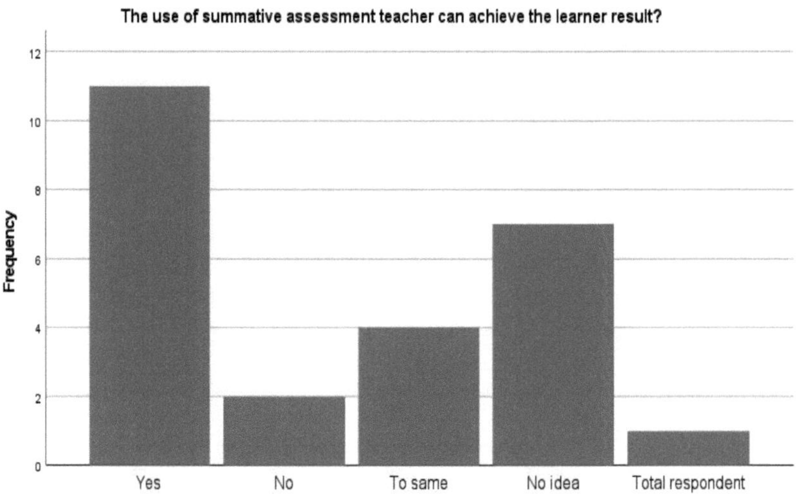

The use of summative assessment teacher can achieve the learner result?

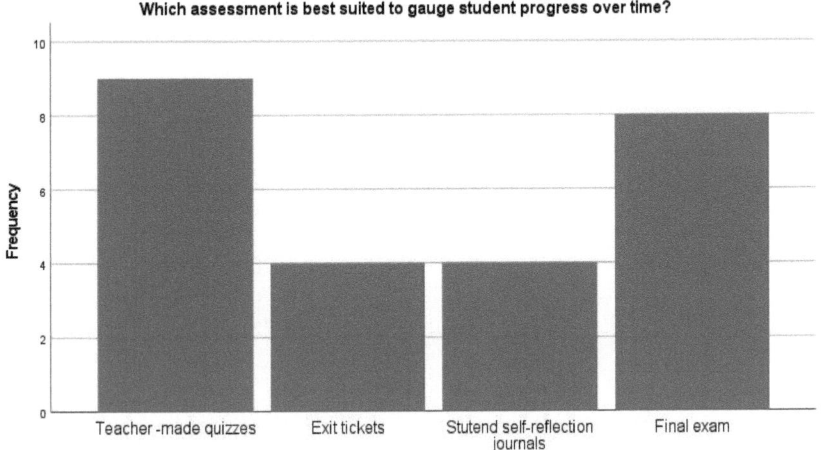

Which assessment is best suited to gauge student progress over time?

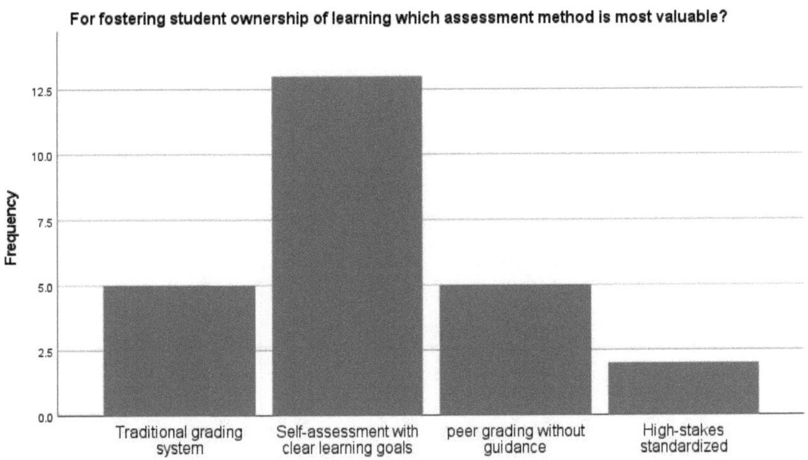

For fostering student ownership of learning which assessment method is most valuable?

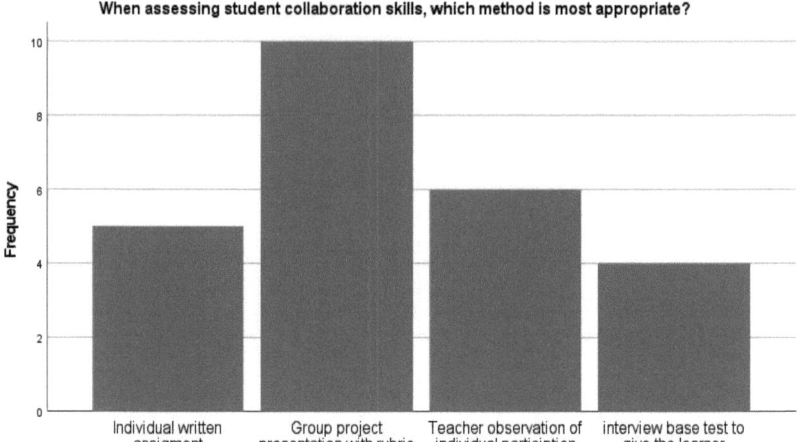

When assessing student collaboration skills, which method is most appropriate?

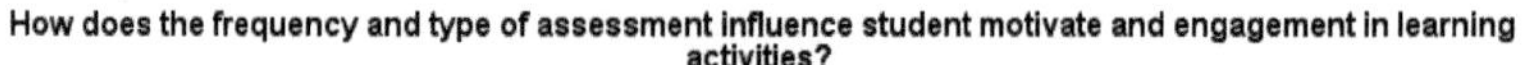

How does the frequency and type of assessment influence student motivate and engagement in learning activities?

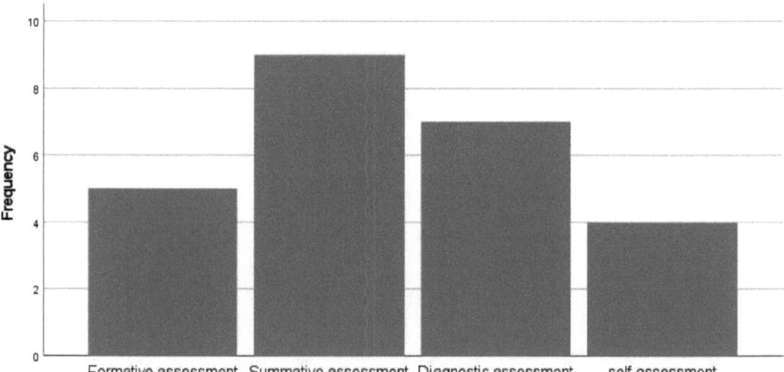

How does the frequency and type of assessment influence student motivate and engagement in learning activities?

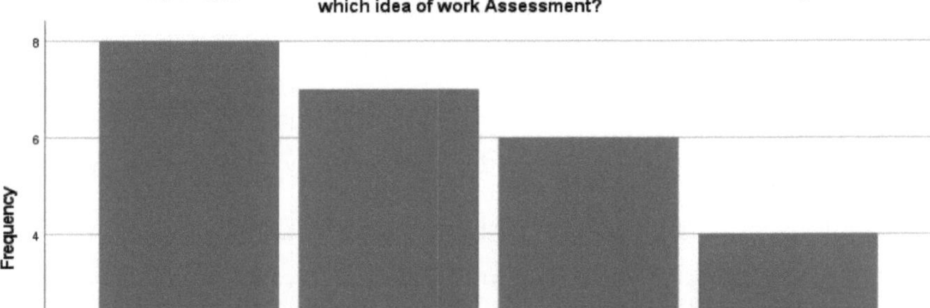

How does the frequency peer assessment help for the development of learner abilities through the use of which idea of work Assessment?

4.24 RESULTS OF STUDY

The data analysis carried out was organized into ten different themes. The findings of the study were as follow and also develop the new ideas that how to use the assessment in primary level school and also improved the ideas and also the teacher follow the assessment method to improve the learner skills and clear the doubts of teacher and student the use the assessment method.

4.24.1 Motivated Students

Based on the study, using tabs for student assessment encouraged students to attend class regularly and show interest in both the teaching-learning process and classroom activities through effective motivation.

CHAPTER NO 5

SUMMARY, FINDINGS, C0NCLUTION, DISCUSSION

5.1 Summary

This is in line with previous research findings which noted that while formative assessment is desirable, it is not easy for teachers to achieve (Torrance and Pryor 2001; Hall and Burke 2003; James et al. 2007). The difficulty in effective implementation could partly be attributed to the fact that, for the teachers in our study, formative assessment does not yet represent a well-defined set of practices. As Bennett (2011) argues some of these misunderstandings, difficulties and practical challenges that teachers face derive from residual ambiguity in the definitions of the formative assessment. The teachers usually tended to be embracing the concept, but in reality implementing a set of practices that were rather mechanical without the active engagement of their students.

Based on the framework developed in the study, a number of weaknesses in teachers' formative assessment practices and understanding have been identified. Firstly, teachers demonstrated a lack of quality criteria and could not make explicit what the purpose of certain activities was and what would count as doing them well. Even in cases where there were criteria, the teachers failed in most cases to make those criteria explicit. Teachers underlined this finding by saying that they often had no clear Educ Asse Eval Acc (2014) 26:153–176 169 idea of the criteria by which they assess, and could not easily spell them out. A possible explanation would be that most of the assignments and tasks are being taken out of the school textbooks in a rather mechanistic procedure. However, according to Torrance (2001), the time spent articulating criteria at the beginning of an activity can mean less 'trouble-shooting' later as they became a focal point of feedback which the teacher build on and underline their importance.

80

5.2 Finding regarding perception of teachers about investigation the effectiveness of different assessment method in primary school classroom in Islamabad.

1. Table 4.1 describe that (56%) had totally age is above then 18 or that teacher of different sector school participation in investigation the effectiveness of different assessment In primary school classroom. While (28%) had totally age of (16%) the table value of mean score is (28.0) is greater and favoure the statement. Whereas, the cumulative percent (100.0) .

2. Table 4.2 describe that (84%) had totally M is above the 18 or that teacher of different sector school participation Gender. While (16%) had totally age of (84%) the table value of mean score is (16.0 is greater and favoure the statement. Whereas, the cumulative percent (100.0) at Significance level. Hence it was founded that the statement is accepted.

3. Table 4.3 describe that (76. %) had totally that teacher of different sector school participation your resignation. While (24%) had totally student (76%) the table value of mean score is 76.0 is greater and favoure the statement. Whereas, the cumulative percent (100.0) at Significance level. Hence it was founded that the statement is accepted.

4. Table 4.4 describe that the teacher (60%) are married the totally the teacher the (40%) percent are unmarried or the totally the all participation marital status. Valid percent (60%) and while the table value 100.0.

Table 4.6 describe that the (8%) teacher are never use the assessment or (12%) teacher rarely use assessment and the totally the all teacher are (25%) and the In your opinion, the assessment is most effective for identifying student strength and weaknesses the (16%) teacher use it sometime or the (20%) frequently use it or the (44%) teacher always use the assessment method in classroom or the totally all 100.0 or the valid percent. 44 or the cumulative percent is 100.

5.3 Conclusion

This is in line with previous research findings which noted that while formative assessment is desirable, it is not easy for teachers to achieve (Torrance and Pryor 2001; Hall and Burke 2003; James et al. 2007). The difficulty in effective implementation could partly be attributed to the fact that, for the teachers in our study, formative assessment does not yet represent a well-defined set of practices. As Bennett (2011) argues some of these misunderstandings, difficulties and practical challenges that teachers face derive from residual ambiguity in the definitions of the formative assessment. The teachers usually tended to be embracing the concept, but in reality implementing a set of practices that were rather mechanical without the active engagement of their students.

Based on the framework developed in the study, a number of weaknesses in teachers' formative assessment practices and understanding have been identified. Firstly, teachers demonstrated a lack of quality criteria and could not make explicit what the purpose of certain activities was and what would count as doing them well. Even in cases where there were criteria, the teachers failed in most cases to make those criteria explicit..

Teachers underlined this finding by saying that they often had no clear Educ Asse Eval Acc (2014) 26:153–176 169 idea of the criteria by which they assess, and could not easily spell them out. A possible explanation would be that most of the assignments and tasks are being taken out of the school textbooks in a rather mechanistic procedure. However, according to Torrance (2001), the time spent articulating criteria at the beginning of an activity can mean less 'trouble-shooting' later as they became a focal point of feedback which the teacher build on and underline their importance.

5.4 Discussion

It is widely reported that use of information and communication technologies in education plays an important role in development of a knowledgeable society. As technology becomes more accessible globally, education systems are also subject to revolution (Chen, Cheng, Chang, Zheng & Huang, 2014). The research was instituted to probe the answers to the questions that how teachers use tabs in student assessment and what are the benefits of using tabs for teachers.

The study was conducted by taking interviews with primary school teachers or given them questionnaire. Different themes were generated based on the data collected through interviews with teachers (guviend, 2010)"The individual interview is a process of data collection in qualitative research in which the researcher asks the questions and records the responses of a single participant in the study at the same time" (Creswell, 2008, p. 226).

It originated in the study that the use of the tabs motivates students to come to school and improves their learning, this is supported by the results of the study conducted by Barry (2014), also found that the use of tabs helps students in their learning. 172 EDUC, ASSE, (2014) 26:153–176 It must be noted that it is not the intent of this study to deliver any kind of final statements on the teachers' practices and rationale of formative assessment in every educational setting. To attempt to do so would be to fall prey to several fallacies, not the least of which is the failure to recognize the context-dependent nature of every classroom, every teacher-student relationship. The four participating teachers are particular to their time and place and certainly do not represent all teachers in Cyprus.

Although no legitimate attempt can be made to make generalizations from these data, overall, the findings of this study may suggest trends and approaches that could lend themselves to a more precise definition and improvement of formative assessment in the future. It is in this explanatory vein that the report of the findings and their interpretations is made.

.

REFERENCE

Andrade. (2010). *Teacher and classroom assessment* .

2017, A. a. (2017). *ClASSROOM ASSESSMENT* . Sweden .

Al.2012, b. e. (2012). *classroom assessment* . kingston.

Bennett. (2013). *CLSSROOM ASSESSMENT* . USA.

Briggs et al.2012, N. 2. (2012). *classroom assassment* . Kingston,notwithstanding

D. M. (2009). *classroom based learing.*

Dick, N. M. (2009.2006). *farmative and summative assessment.*

Fulcher, l. (2012,2014). *teacher and classroom assessment* .

S. S. (2005). *research artical.* islamabad.

2011, e. B. (2011). *Classroom assessment* .

2014, V. a.-P. (2014). *Classroom assessment* . nowithstanding .

2017, A. a. (2017). *ClASSROOM ASSESSMENT* . Sweden .

al.2012, b. e. (2012). *classroom assessment* . kingston.

cheng, w. (2005,2001). *Role of CBA in language Acquisition.*

joues, B. a. (2008,2007). *farmative and summative assessment.*

kenan, W. a. (2004,2006). *classroom Based assessment in pakistan.*

lyte, C.-S. a. (2011). *classroom assessment* .

nowell. (2017).

perron. (2011). *Research artical* .

pestieau, G. a. (1995). classroom assessment . *Research artical.*

purpure. (2009). *language Study* .

Redickens. (2008). *Role of CBA language acquisition.*

shute, H. a. (2007,2007). *classroom assessment* .

thompson, w. a. (2008). *farmative assessment.*

Villegas-Reimers, R. (2003.2003). *Research artical.*

waris 2004, M. 2. (2004,2012). *Artical* . ISALAMABAD .

Warsi, K. (2004,2006). *Classroom Based Assessment in Pakistan.*

wiliam 1998. (2013). *previous Research on classroom assessment* . islamabad .

Willams. (1998). *Research artical.*

Appendix-A

<u>**QUESTIONNER FOR TEACHERS.**</u>

<u>Dear Teacher,</u>

I am student of BS Education at International Islamic University Islamabad. My research topic is. Effectiveness of different assessment method in primary school classroom in Islamabad. I collect the data. In this regard, one questionnaire is dispatched. Can you place spare 20 minute to fill it out? I shall thankful for your cooperation.

Yours truly

Shah Fahad

BS student,

IIUI

Name (optional): —————————— Name of school ——————————

Gender: ——————————

Please read the statement carefully and tick ( ) the mostly appropriate option.

Totally Frequently= FY Always = Aw Sometime= ST

Statements					
In your opinion, the formative assessment is most effective for identifying student strength and weaknesses?					
How often do you use peer assessment that student evaluate in your classroom to each other?					
How self, assessment method develop collaboration between in the student evaluate, each other?					

How often do you use diagnostic assessment during the class to observe your student pervious knowledge?					
How often do you use summative assessment at the end of subject or topic (e.g. Quizzes, project). In your classroom?					
Do you use, combination of assessment method at a same time or you get well, rounded picture of student learning?					
DO you find assessment method more effective for certain subject?					
How the assessment method used and motivate student and promote a growth of leaners?					
Through the use of assessment method do you take engage the student in class work?					
When implementing different assessment method how do you consider drives method drivers learning style and abilities in your classroom?					
Assessment method can effect on primary level school student?					
How often do you communicate assessment result with parents or group works?					
In your opinion, how effective are performance-based assessments in measuring student understanding?					

Investigation the effectiveness of different assessment in primary school classroom in lslamabad.					
Do performance based assessment encourage deeper learning and critical thinking skills?					
How often do you involve students in self-assessment activities?					
Do you believe self-assessment helps students become weaknesses?					

Are there any challenges you face when implementing different assessment method?					
Do you differentiate your assessment based on student learning style?					
Do formative assessment provide immediate feedback to students?					
The use of assessment method can develop the learning environment?					
How the assessment method gives learner opportunity th learner?					
Do the assessment help the teacher to measure the pupil abilities?					
The use of summative assessment teacher can achieve the learner result?					

Printed by Books on Demand GmbH, Norderstedt / Germany